BLESSED ARE THEY THAT MOURN

THE WOMEN AT THE TOMB
BY FRA ANGELICO

"I am the Resurrection and the Life: he that believeth in Me, although he be dead, shall live."
ST. JOHN XI:25

"Catholic literature, doctrinal and devotional, owes a great deal to Mother Mary Loyola. There is a certain wholesomeness, naturalness, geniality about her spirituality that at once wins a place in the Catholic heart for whatever she writes." --The Ecclesiastical Review, volume 58, January 1918

About Mother Mary Loyola:

Most Catholics today who have heard the name Mother Mary Loyola know her as the author of *The King of the Golden City*, which has enjoyed a resurgence in popularity in recent years. But few know that she wrote over two dozen works, and that she was once a household name among Catholics of her era. What made her unique among Catholic authors was her ability to draw in her listeners with story after story—and not just any stories, but ones that incorporated current events and brand new inventions of the time. Despite the fact that those events are no longer current, and those inventions no longer brand new, her books scintillate with the appeal of an active mind that could find a moral in the most unusual places. And while the printed word lacks the animated facial expressions and vocal inflections which reveal a gifted storyteller, hers convey her enthusiasm so capably that the reader can easily imagine sitting at the feet of this wise old nun.

About *Blessed are they that Mourn*:

By the early years of the twentieth century, Mother Mary Loyola had cemented her reputation as one of the best Catholic writers of her generation, but the First World War prompted her to write a book of consolation for the innumerable mothers, wives and others who had lost loved ones to its ravages. Her intimate knowledge of the subject matter gave her unique insight, for she had lost so many in the course of her long life, beginning with both of her parents and two siblings when she was just nine years old, and recently including several of her own beloved students who were fighting in the trenches of the Great War. She knew only too well the need for a strong faith in these times of intense suffering and loss, and this she amply illustrates in *Blessed are they that Mourn*.

To learn more about Mother Mary Loyola, visit our website at **www.staugustineacademypress.com.**

BLESSED
ARE THEY THAT
MOURN

BY
MOTHER MARY LOYOLA
OF THE BAR CONVENT YORK

EDITED BY
HERBERT THURSTON, S.J.

2011
ST. AUGUSTINE ACADEMY PRESS
LISLE, ILLINOIS

NIHIL OBSTAT:

H. S. Bowden. *Censor deputatus.*

IMPRIMATVR:

Edm. Can. Surmont. *Vic. Gen.*

Westmonasterii, die 7 Decembris 1916.

This book was originally published in 1917 by Burns & Oates. This edition ©2011 by St. Augustine Academy Press. All editing by Lisa Bergman.

ISBN: 978-1-936639-04-5
Library of Congress Control Number: 2011941818

TO THE MOURNERS OF THE GREAT WAR
WHOSE SACRIFICE IN THE CAUSE OF
CHRISTIANITY HUMANITY AND JUSTICE
ALL WHO COME AFTER US WILL ACKNOWLEDGE
WITH REVERENT SYMPATHY
& DEEPEST GRATITUDE

CONTENTS

Editor's Note:

In presenting this edition, I have attempted to be as faithful as possible to the original text of Mother Mary Loyola's *Blessed are they that Mourn* as printed by Burns and Oates in 1917. Numerous errors in the text and especially in the footnotes made this a very difficult task. Therefore, I was forced to make some minor editorial changes in order to correct these errors where possible and to make clear what I perceived the original intent to be. I have not changed any of what Mother Loyola wrote; I have merely corrected egregious errors of spelling, punctuation and in the citation of Bible verses. I chose, however, to retain the style of the original citations, though it is different from what we are used to seeing.

Lastly, I would point out that all Scriptural references found in this book are from the Catholic Douay-Rheims version, and thus they often do not align in chapter and verse with modern bibles, which conform more closely to the chapter and verse structure of the Protestant King James version.

In Christ,
Lisa Bergman
St. Augustine Academy Press
April 2011

PREFACE

THERE are many, it is to be feared, in these evil times who find the text, "Blessed are they that mourn," to be a hard saying, an utterance against which weak human nature protests and revolts. Anguish of heart, when allied with action in a noble cause, or even with any form of profitable endurance, has its own compensations; but the mere role of the mourner, whose suffering helps not, and the intensity of whose pain transcends immeasurably any outward manifestations consistent with self-respect, is apt to overwhelm the spirit and to crush it to earth. Too often the poor sufferer hugs her sorrow almost selfishly as a precious souvenir, or as though it were indeed the phantom of him whom she has lost. Shakespeare, who has sounded the depths of all human emotion, paints for us an unforgettable picture of a mother's bereavement in KING JOHN. "You are as fond of grief as of your son," protests King Philip to the distraught Constance. To which she answers:

> "Grief fills the room up of my absent child,
> Lies in his bed, walks up and down with me,
> Puts on his pretty looks, repeats his words,
> Remembers me of all his gracious parts,
> Stuffs out his vacant garments with his form,
> Then have I reason to be fond of grief."

It is Mother Mary Loyola's kindly purpose in the pages which follow to offer her tribute of deepest and most respectful sympathy to the many wives, mothers, daughters, sisters or betrothed whose cup of sorrow has been filled brim-full by the terrible happenings of the war. But she gives them more than barren sympathy, she provides substantial comfort, as well as help to guide their thoughts heavenward to the one and only source of consolation. "He talks to me that never had a son," was the stricken mother's answer when Pandulph bade her moderate her grief. It was an apt retort and carries weight. But I do not think that those who read the words of comfort which Mother Mary Loyola has printed in this little volume will find them lacking in perception of the true gravity of the hurts she tries to assuage. There is, it seems to me, a wonderful gentleness of touch in her probing of the wound, and her diffidence as to her own power of finding the apt and helpful word is evidenced by her constant and almost exaggerated recourse to scriptural examples and by her retention everywhere of the actual phraseology of Holy Writ. The wish to be of use to non-Catholic readers has also operated in the same direction, for the undertaking of this little book was originally pressed upon her as a service to be rendered to the too numerous class of them who sorrow "even as others who have no hope." What Mother Mary Loyola contributes of her own is a glow of sympathy and an idealisation of abstract right, hardly possible outside convent walls, but helpful at the same time to those of us whose contact with the more sordid side of life often leads to a belittling of much that is noble in human action and stimulating in human purpose. One might appeal especially to sections xiv and vi, entitled respectively, "Women receive their Dead raised to Life," and "Some more Valiant Ones," as particularly characteristic of the author's method and point of view.

But in sum the consolation which Mother Loyola offers is a very simple one based upon the bed-rock of Christian faith and hope. She bids the mourner look upon our Lord Jesus Christ, "who having joy set before Him, endured the cross despising the shame," and find in Him and Him alone the courage and graces that are necessary. It is only the "Sis ipse nostrum gaudium" of the Ascension hymn, thus happily paraphrased by Mother Francis Raphael in her "Songs in the Night."

> Where should we lift our weeping eyes
>   But only unto Thee,
> That Thou who art our future prize
>   Our present joy may be?

Mother Loyola's touching little volume is one, I feel sure, which will bring balm to many a sorely stricken heart.

Herbert Thurston, S.J.

31 Farm Street,
Oct. 22nd, 1916.

THE MARTYRDOM OF THE SEVEN MACCABEES
by Antonio Ciseri

I
VALIANT ONES

IN the Collect for Virgin Martyrs—that class of the Blessed which was Cardinal Newman's special admiration and envy—the Church praises God for "giving even to the weaker sex the victory of martyrdom." Women and children stand, or did stand, for the helpless and downtrodden, things of small account therefore, in the judgment of "the wicked... for that which is feeble is found to be nothing worth."[1] Yet they hold a foremost rank among "the weak things of the world which God has chosen that He may confound the strong,"[2] and from the first they have given to the Church examples of heroic fortitude as confessors or as martyrs.

In the great women of Scripture, the quality singled out by the word of God for special admiration is valour. Is it because the disproportion between the instrument and the work it achieves is such glory to Him who employs it? In the Old Testament we find Jahel, and Judith and Esther; the valiant woman who "put out her hand to strong things,"[3] and the mother of the seven martyrs in the persecution of Antiochus Epiphanes. In the Gospel, we have the women who followed our Lord with their lamentations when all others forsook Him, the three who stood beneath His Cross to the last, and those who on the third day

1 Wisdom ii. 11.
2 I Cor i. 27.
3 Prov. xxxi. 19.

braved the darkness, the earthquake, and the Roman guards, to give Him the last tokens of their devotedness at the sepulchre. Of one of these He had said that her devotion to Him in the face of general opposition should be told in memory of her wherever the Gospel should be preached.

Among these valiant ones, two stand out pre-eminent, one in the Old Dispensation, the other in the New—two mothers, and both pierced with a seven-fold sword. Of one we are told that her seven sons were put to death by atrocious tortures—"the mother looking on."[1] Of the other, "there stood by the cross of Jesus His Mother."[2] In both cases it is the valour of endurance that is recorded for the admiration of all ages. Beside it, the prowess of Jahel and of Judith fades into insignificance. Their intrepid deeds involved no anguish to those dear to them. But these suffered in those whose lives were immeasurably dearer to them than their own. The mother of seven martyr sons was martyred seven times over before she offered her own life. She "beheld her seven sons slain in the space of one day...Last of all after the sons the mother also was consumed," and her martyrdom was over. The anguish of the other Mother, whose love for her Son exceeded that of all mothers, was not of one day. Calvary was but the consummation of the sacrifice begun in the Temple with the prophecy of Simeon three and thirty years before. She tended her Child from His birth, as a victim for sacrifice. She saw him grow up as the "Man of Sorrows." The hour of His immolation was always before her eyes. Nor must we think her loss on Calvary was of three days only, mitigated therefore to a very large extent by the knowledge that it would be shortly repaid beyond measure by the restoration of all she had sacrificed. The Crucifixion was indeed followed by the Resurrection, but that again by the Ascension and the long weary years of waiting for the eternal reunion in Heaven.

1   II Mach vii. 4
2   S. John xix. 25

3

It is this martyrdom of the heart that so many today are called to share. Our Lord saw it all from His cross. He looked down, not merely on the bereavement and anguish of the little band below, who in losing Him were losing their all, but out far beyond. He was God as well as Man. He saw all the ages to come and every heart that sorrow was to rend. Every national calamity, every pain that was to befall those whom He loved to call His brethren, passed through His heart in Gethsemane as He lay beneath the olive trees, "sorrowful even unto death." He has made Himself one of us, and His greatest desire is to share with us all that He can share, our sorrows above all. He knows them every one. He knows pain of body and distress of mind by that way which appeals to us most—experience. "Surely He hath borne our infirmities and carried our sorrows."[1] "The whole head is sick and the whole heart is sad."[2] Sick and sad, that He may be able to give to us one by one the undivided sympathy of His sacred Human Heart. He knows by experience what anguish the heart can endure—the torture of anticipation, the shock and the pain when the blow falls, the prostration and the desolation that follow.

All this He knows, and not as the most sympathising of our friends know it—they can but guess at best. He knows us through and through, better far than we know ourselves. "But not by experience," someone will say. Yes, by experience. "He hath carried our sorrows," is true, not only of the sufferings mentioned by the Evangelists, but of each personal sorrow of every one of us. We may not say: "In such a multitude I shall not be known, for what is my soul in such an immense creation?"[3] "For He hath set His eye upon our hearts,"[4] "and every heart is understood by Him."[5] More keenly, more affectionately,

1   Isaias liii. 4
2   Isaias i. 5
3   Ecclus. xvi. 17.
4   Ecclus. xvii. 7.
5   Ecclus. xvi. 20.

than mother, wife or sister are sharing now the sorrow of their nearest and dearest, has the tender Heart of Christ taken to itself all your experiences, whether of sorrow or of joy. He can no longer suffer, but the affection and the sympathy with which He once bore your pain of this hour He retains—"Jesus, yesterday, to-day, and the same for ever."[1]

Yet we have this to bear in mind. Sympathy is the fellow-feeling of friends. If there is anything in my dispositions which my divine Friend cannot share, it will be a hindrance to His sympathy and to the strength and consolation He desires my heart should receive from His. The Cross that weighs so heavily on thousands of hearts and homes to-day is being met in very different ways, the difference being due to the greater or less faith of those to whom it comes. If faith is weak, sorrow may embitter. If faith is robust, trial will result in fortitude here, and in the peace "which passeth all understanding," in company with those we love, hereafter.

We may distinguish three classes of mourners in this War—those who have no hope, that is, those who are without faith—these may rebel: those who have faith sufficient to bear the Cross without murmuring, but not enough to reap the fruit which greater generosity would have brought them: those whose faith has led them to see this dispensation of God in its twofold aspect, as a visitation of justice on the one hand, and of tenderest mercy on the other, as in the widespread arms of the Crucifix we see the divine wrath angered by sin, and the Friend of sinners calling to His embrace all who suffer and are heavy burdened that He may refresh them.

We know of course what Christians understand by the cross. But there is no harm in reminding ourselves. The cross is not mere suffering. It is suffering sanctified by the touch of Christ as the Church says of the sacred wood on Passion Sunday—

1 Heb. xiii. 8.

Arbor decora et fulgida
Ornata regis purpura,
Electa digno stipite
Tam sancta membra tangere.

O comely tree! thou radiant bride!
By kingly purple sanctified,
Thou chosen from a high-born race
God's hallowed members to embrace.

The cross is suffering offered to us by Christ, that as His members we may suffer with our Head.

The new doctrine regarding suffering brought in by the Reformers of the 16th century was utterly subversive of the Christian instinct which, under the guidance of the Church, had hitherto prevailed. Our Lord and His Apostles had taught that "Christ suffered for us, leaving us an example that we should follow His steps."[1] The Head was to lead the members on the road of suffering, not to exempt them. He suffered enough and more than enough for our "plentiful redemption," but not to set us free to take our fill of pleasure with that crushed and bleeding Figure before our eyes. The men who swept away the crucifying fast and abstinence, the crucifying vows of religion, the whole discipline of penance with its restraints on mind and body, did so on the plea that Christ, having done all for us in the way of satisfaction and merit, had left nothing for us to do for ourselves: that to rely on His merits whilst we do nothing to deserve them, and presume to add none of our own; to take advantage of our membership with Him to secure future glory whilst shirking present pain; in a word, to leave Him to suffer alone—this is to prove loyalty and love and to glorify His redemption.

How different is the teaching He Himself has left us: "The disciple is not above the master, nor the servant above his lord."[2] "If any man will come after Me, let him deny himself,

---

1   I Peter ii. 21.
2   S. Matt. x. 24.

and take up his cross and follow Me."[1] "I say to you, unless you do penance you shall all perish."[2] Following this teaching, the Apostles made it abundantly clear to their converts "that through many tribulations we must enter into the Kingdom of God."[3]

But had there been no other comment on our Lord's words than the reminder of St. Paul: "Now you are the body of Christ, and members of member. If one member suffer anything, all the members suffer with it; or if one member glory, all the members rejoice with it,"[4] this would suffice. This is the doctrine of loving fellowship which accounts for the heroic suffering of martyrs, confessors, and all the servants of Christ. Forgetfulness of it brought about the laxity of which history is full. But it was reserved for the Reformers of the 16th century, not only to encourage laxity and moral evil of every kind, but to glorify it with the sanction of religion. To "hold fast the faith once delivered to the saints,"[5] does not, alas! suffice to make us what we should be; but it is certain that according to the firmness of our grasp of truth will be the strength of our union with Christ as members of His body.

For this reason the Church has always sought to keep before her faithful the image of Christ crucified. When the Iconoclasts struck at it, she anathematized them, and her martyrs died in its defence. She knows the value of its silent teaching. It is the one sufficient answer to that question of suffering which perplexes the minds of so many. "Why did our Saviour suffer?" our Catechism asks. "Our Saviour suffered to atone for our sins and to purchase for us eternal life." As His members, we have to follow where He has led. We, too, have to suffer to atone for our sins, His Atonement giving value to ours by the one

1 S. Matt. xvi. 24.
2 S. Luke xiii. 3.
3 Acts xiv. 21.
4 I Cor. xii. 27, 26.
5 S. Jude i. 3.

life vivifying the Head and the members. We have to "work out our salvation"[1] and merit eternal life by applying to our souls the merits of Christ by which alone our works can be of efficacy for Heaven. In this way we are to "fill up those things that are wanting in the sufferings of Christ,"[2] "bearing about in our body the mortification of Jesus, that the life also of Jesus may be made manifest in our bodies;"[3] "knowing that as you are partakers of the sufferings," says St. Paul, "so shall you be also of the consolation."[4] And he concludes: "That I may know Him and the power of His resurrection, and the fellowship of His sufferings, being made conformable to His death. If by any means I may attain to the resurrection which is from the dead."[5] How earnestly does the great Apostle, who, on his own showing, had suffered more than the others, strive to bring home to his converts that they must suffer with Christ here to rejoice with Him hereafter! Future reward had to be kept prominently before them to sustain their hope and courage in the fierce persecutions through which they were passing. Death was continually before their eyes; the Resurrection of Christ as the model of their own had to be brought before them constantly, as we see from the rude frescoes of the catacombs. During those early times the Cross with its associated shame was not indeed forgotten, for the perils of each day reminded them of it, but it was veiled. On the other hand, the types of the Resurrection were multiplied, and believers were reminded at every turn of Christ's promise that they should reign with Him hereafter.

In the Crucifix we see the suffering that is to be rewarded and glorified presently. We see the justice of God, and His tenderest love; the chastisement of sin, and the embrace waiting for the

1   Phil. ii. 12.
2   Coloss. i. 24.
3   II Cor. iv. 10.
4   II Cor. i. 7.
5   Philip. iii. 10-11.

sinner, the warning, the encouragement, and the comfort our poor world needs to-day.

"Where is God? How can there be a God to allow such frightfulness?" some are asking. "Surely there must be a God in Heaven," say others, "and sin must be a frightful thing to account for this deluge of evils which has come upon us. There must be another life in which the wrongs we see to-day will be righted, the innocent and the helpless avenged, and the wicked punished; a life of happiness and of glory to reward the lives so nobly sacrificed at the call of duty."

Here is faith bringing about that acknowledgment of God's sovereignty and justice which leads to the confession of our sinfulness and humble submission to its chastisement: "We have sinned and committed iniquity, departing from Thee... Wherefore all that Thou hast brought upon us and everything Thou hast done to us, Thou hast done in true judgement... Nevertheless, in a contrite heart and humble spirit let us be accepted."[1]

God forbid that we should ever give entrance to thoughts of disloyalty or resentment against Him who created us for eternal happiness with Himself. But temptation may rush in upon any one of us, especially in time of trial. We have all sinned, and the unhappy consequence of sin is to dull the understanding and warp the will, so that not only do we fail to see the hand of God in the evils that come upon us, but when we do recognise it, we are stirred to indignation and complaint. By sin we wander away from God's standpoint where things are seen in their true light and proportion. We substitute our own, and judge of all that happens by the way in which it affects ourselves. What brings us pleasure we approve. So long as God's Will coincides with our own, we are content to bless and praise Him. But the moment His just chastisement for sin touches us, or His

---

1   Dan. iii. 29, 31, 39.

far-seeing love mingles pain with our pleasure, lest the good things of this life should make us lose those which are eternal— we rebel. And forthwith we lose our peace. "For who hath resisted Him and hath had peace?"[1] "Peace is the tranquillity of order."[2] To recover it we must readjust things; move back to the true standpoint; remember that we are creatures, for whom dependence on our Creator is at once the first of our duties and the only solid consolation in our sufferings. "You have said: The way of the Lord is not right...Is it My way that is not right, and are not rather your ways perverse?...Be converted and do penance...and make to yourselves a new heart and a new spirit: why will you die, O House of Israel?"[3]

We may notice that it is only in what directly or indirectly concerns ourselves that this distortion of view has place. We are ready enough to see, and even to call for, the intervention of Divine Justice when there is question of the misdeeds of others; ready, even, to see God's merciful designs in sending affliction, when we have to console our sorrowing friends. But when trouble knocks at our own door all is changed. "Behold, thou hast taught many, and thou hast strengthened the weary hands; thy words have confirmed them that were staggering, and thou hast strengthened the trembling knees. But now the scourge has come upon thee and thou faintest; it hath touched thee and thou art troubled."[4] This is the experience of us all. Trouble, which we can prove to be so profitable to others, is an unmixed evil when it touches ourselves. How is it we forget that for us, too, God is not only our Creator, but our All Wise and most Loving Father, who has our good at heart far more than we have it ourselves, and is leading us and those we love to a happiness which will surpass our most extravagant

1   Job ix. 4.
2   S. Thomas Aquinas
3   Ezech. xviii. 25, 30, 31.
4   Job iv. 5.

expectation and desire. But as to the road thither, we must trust His Wisdom and fall in with His designs for us.

By reason of His supreme rights, He might, like earthly sovereigns, have required us to serve Him at our own cost. This He never does. All that happens is as much designed, or permitted, for our good, as if this were the sole end He had in view. Nothing happens to us by chance. We are sacrificed to no other more beloved. Every detail of our life, and of the lives of others, so far as it affects us, has been foreseen by Him from eternity and deliberately chosen, or permitted, as a means of securing to us the eternal happiness He has in store for us. We have to make our acts of faith as to this. We have to combat the rebellion, or resentment, or mistrust which refuses to believe in the reality of a love it is too sore to try to understand. Oh that we could do more than combat! Or rather, that combat were not called for, that we had the loyalty, the childlike trust which no shock can disturb, no trial disconcert. Faith and trust have a wonderful power to call forth the admiration and praise of God Himself: "O woman, great is thy faith."[1] "Now the mother was to be admired above measure and worthy to be remembered by good men, who beheld her seven sons slain in the space of one day, and bore it with a good courage, for the hope that she had in God."[2]

Of the rich and prosperous Job we read that upon a certain day messenger after messenger rushed in upon him bringing word that all his cattle and servants were slain "by the fire of God that fell from heaven," or by the sword of enemies. The third messenger "was yet speaking, and behold another came in and said: Thy sons and daughters were eating and drinking in the house of their elder brother; a violent wind came on a sudden and shook the four corners of the house, and it fell upon thy children and they are dead, and I alone have escaped

1   S. Matth. xv. 28.
2   II Mach. vii. 20.

to tell thee. Then Job rose up, and rent his garments, and fell down upon the ground and worshipped, and said...the Lord gave, and the Lord hath taken away; as it hath pleased the Lord so be it done; blessed be the name of the Lord. In all these things Job sinned not by his lips, nor spoke he any foolish thing against God."[1]

Observe—he does not distinguish between the disasters that come direct from God, "the fire from heaven," and the "violent wind," and those that are due to the malice of men. All was from heaven, sent or permitted: "blessed be the name of the Lord." His resignation was perfect, yet it did not blunt the anguish. The shock overthrew him. He rose up and rent his garments, and fell down upon the ground: *and worshipped.* The very force of the blow drove him to his God. "In all these things Job sinned not by his lips, nor spoke he any foolish thing against God." Wrath, resistance, murmuring are here condemned as foolishness, short-sighted folly flying in the face of eternal Wisdom and Love. Prostrated by the extremity of his misery, Job fell down upon the ground, and worshipped. Not simply accepted the Will of God, but worshipped It!

And this before the Incarnation had taught us the tender love of our Heavenly Father for us; before men knew that "God so loved the world as to give His Only-begotten Son that the world maybe saved by Him"[2]; "that as Man He would suffer with us as well as for us; as Man bear the loss of all things the heart holds dear, and, sorrowful unto death," teach us to say: "Father, if this chalice may not pass from me, Thy Will be done!"

---

1   Job i. 18-22.
2   S. John iii. 16, 17.

THE CROSS IN THE MOUNTAINS

by Caspar David Friedrich

II

"THE SIGN OF THE SON OF MAN"
Renew Thy signs and work new miracles.—Ecclus. xxxvi., 6.

B UT some will say: "I have not the power to quell the rebellion in my heart. Why has the light been taken out of my life? Why am I so cruelly stricken when others are spared? The agony of my loss crushes me. Past, present, future—it is all pain, pain, pain. And I rebel, or sink down like Rachel in hopeless misery. Till my loss is made good to me, there can be no consolation for me, and I desire none. Do not speak to me of submission and trust. I cannot make the effort."

Yes, you can. With God's help you can make that little move towards Him which will open the way to further grace. Try. He will meet you more than half way. Try—and you will find the wall between you and Him crumbling down; your heart softening; His grace entering; courage returning. Then will come the brave resolve to set yourself loyally on His side by meek acceptance of His Will, patience, and trust.

In return He promises you His peace, "the peace of God which surpasseth all understanding."[1] You will learn what is a mystery now, that peace is consistent with the heaviest cross; that it is found, not in the fulfilment of our desires, but in the cleaving of our will to His. We find peace even in the act of humbling ourselves under His chastening hand. We are sinners and deserve chastisement. This we know. We know, too, that

---

1   Philip. iv. 7.

as strangers and pilgrims in this world, we cannot expect the full satisfaction of all our desires and affections which awaits us at Home. Our way is necessarily beset with hardships and trial. Sooner or later sorrow must come to us all. But that suffering has a special mission of purification and preparation for God's specially beloved ones; that patient suffering, "momentary and light,"[1] will have eternal consolation, exceeding all expectation and desire; that "because thou wert acceptable to God it was necessary that temptation," that is trial, "should prove thee"[2]— oh, it is well with us when we come to realise this! Realising it, shall we grieve overmuch that this mark of divine predilection is upon our lives?

But why is there this necessity for suffering?

Because the cross, which was the chosen instrument of our Redemption, is likewise God's chosen means for the sanctification of all the elect. Even in the natural order there is something wanting in the life that sorrow has not yet touched. It gives to man and to woman a refinement, a mellowness, a discernment, a power of sympathy, the absence of which we feel instinctively in the untried. But suffering borne in a Christian spirit, received as our portion of the cross of Christ, the share which as His members we are to bear in the sufferings of our Head, raises us to a still higher plane, to the supernatural order, to that fellowship with Christ in suffering which is to be consummated and rewarded by eternal companionship with Him in glory. This is the transfiguration of suffering, bringing with it even here a serenity and a happiness which this world can neither give nor take away.

Suffering is the portion of all. And it is the test of all. Like Him whose standard it is, the Cross is "set for the rise and for the fall of many." Not in every heart are its saving fruits

---

1   II Cor. iv. 17.
2   Tobias xii. 13.

found. Where there is rebellion or impatience, the purpose of God in sending or permitting affliction is frustrated, resistance to grace set up, peace of mind lost, faith and trust in God dangerously impaired. The burden becomes more and more heavy because unshared, and the poor sufferer complains of the intolerable pressure. Such complaint is not heard where there is submission to God's will. So far from tending to estrange us from God, the Cross draws us to Him if we receive it as we ought. He gives us grace to do this, but He will not force our will. "Thus saith the Lord: Behold, I set before you the way of life and the way of death."[1] It is a choice He is bound to leave with us if we are to be free agents and not slaves; if we are to "work out our salvation" and receive, with eternal happiness, the added joy of its being the fruit of our own labour by co-operation with grace. Let us beseech Him so to aid us that we may choose well and wisely, and in the tests of life set our will loyally alongside of His.

The Cross, then, is the Christian symbol of suffering in its divinely appointed office of fashioning the Church Triumphant by bringing out in the Church Militant that likeness of the members to the Head which will make them worthy of being united with Him for ever in glory. Never, perhaps, has it been forced upon the attention of the world in a more remarkable way than in the present War. Never have the dishonour and the veneration that make up its history been brought together in closer and sharper contrast. Whilst the desecrated sanctuaries of Belgium and of Northern France proclaim the hatred of the "enemies of the cross of Christ,"[2] its wonderful preservation amid the general wreckage—in the churches themselves, in wayside shrines, on the walls of the dilapidated and desolate homes, on the very graves of the ploughed-up cemeteries, is a

---

1   Jerem. xxi. 8.
2   Philip. iii. 18.

consolation to its friends. The men home from the front will tell you eagerly of the "miracle" which protects it amidst the bursting shells on every side.

What is all this but a message from Heaven to us, a call to see in the awful visitation that has overtaken us, God's chastisement of sin, the need of doing penance for our sins, and of accepting in the spirit of penance the sufferings of this life by which we can atone for the past, and merit the rewards promised to penitents?

Is this singular preservation of the Cross which is making such an impression on our men at the front to have no significance for us at home? The Cross has been the herald of great changes in the history of the world. Its appearance or disappearance has changed the destiny of nations. It brought salvation to the world on Calvary. It was shown in the heavens to Constantine as a sign of the overthrow of paganism and of the victory of Christianity. It has carried the good tidings of salvation to every country of East and West. When time has run its course, "the Sign of the Son of Man" will be the distinguishing mark of the elect and save them in the destruction that is to come upon the whole world: "I saw," says St. John, "another Angel ascending from the rising of the sun, having the sign of the living God, and he cried with a loud voice to the four Angels to whom it was given to hurt the earth and the sea, saying: Hurt not the earth and the sea till we sign the servants of our God in their foreheads."[1]

We can hardly fail to notice in the description of the closing scenes of the world's history the continual recurrence of the word "sign." "What shall be the sign of Thy coming and of the consummation of the world?" asked the Apostles. And our Lord made answer: "You shall hear of wars and rumours of wars...Nation shall rise against nation and kingdom against

1   Apoc. vii. 2, 3.

kingdom."[1] "And there shall be great earthquakes in divers places, and pestilences and famines, and terrors from heaven, and there shall be great signs...in the sun and in the moon and in the stars, and upon the earth distress of nations by reason of the confusion of the roaring of the sea and of the waves."[2] "All these are the beginnings of sorrows...And then shall appear the sign of the Son of Man in heaven."[3]

But before that dread Coming He will have signed His own.

God has never withheld from men the signs of coming chastisement. From the beginning it has been His way to multiply such signs in proportion to the severity of the threatened punishment. Our Lord rebuked the Jews of His own time for their hardness of heart in ignoring "the signs of the times." Has He no such rebuke for us? Heaven and earth are teeming with signs. We are on the eve of momentous changes. Men are busy all the world over forecasting and preparing for them. And rightly. But what of the change "which is to come upon the whole world," when men least expect it, and be the overthrow of all projects and policy here? What if the deluge of evils that has come upon the earth—evils which day by day eclipse one another in magnitude and in horror—are indeed "the beginnings of sorrows"? What if the Cross is once again held before the eyes of men for "the rise and fall of many," a "sign to be contradicted," a sign also of salvation and of victory, a sign of the final change!

But now, as in the days of Noe and of Christ, men will refuse the signs of the times and be deaf to warning. "Where are the signs of His coming?" they will be asking, when He is "nigh, even at the doors...For as in the days before the Flood, they were eating and drinking, marrying and giving in marriage even till that day in which Noe entered into the ark, and they

1   S. Matt. xxiv. 6, 7.
2   S. Luke xxi. 11, 25.
3   S. Matt. xxiv. 8, 30.

knew not till the Flood came and took them all away: so also shall the coming of the Son of Man be."[1]

The final words of our Lord's answer to the Apostles' question "What shall be the sign of Thy coming?" are very sad: "Then shall appear the sign of the Son of Man in heaven: and then shall all tribes of the earth mourn."[2] Mourn! when they see at last, and coming in glory, the Cross on which they were redeemed. Mourn! because it announces the Presence and Coming of their Redeemer—oh, how sad it is! Is this the welcome men reserve for Him who loved them unto death, even the death of the cross?

"All tribes of the earth," for, as He Himself tells us, "the Son of Man when He cometh, shall He find, think you, faith on earth?"[3] St. John adds: "Behold He cometh in the clouds and every eye shall see Him...And all the tribes of the earth shall bewail themselves because of Him."[4] Is Redemption, then, a failure? God forbid! The beloved Disciple goes on to say: "After this I saw a great multitude which no man could number, of all nations, and tribes, and peoples, and tongues, standing before the throne and in sight of the Lamb, clothed with white robes, and palms in their hands."[5] And—bear this in mind, for he would have us note it—he saw not only the term of their journey, but the road by which these blessed ones had come. "And one of the ancients answered and said to me: These that are clothed in white robes, who are they? and whence came they? And I said to him: My lord, thou knowest. And he said to me: These are they who are come out of great tribulation, and have washed their robes and have made them white in the blood of the Lamb. Therefore they are before the throne

---

1   S. Matt. xxiv. 33, 38-39.
2   S. Matt. xxiv. 30.
3   S. Luke xviii. 8.
4   Apoc. i. 7.
5   Apoc. vii.9.

of God...They shall no more hunger nor thirst...and God shall wipe away all tears from their eyes."[1]

"Therefore." Because of the "great tribulation," borne in brave submission to the Will of God, they are before His throne, beyond the reach of pain or loss or distress any more. The heart's craving through years of desolation shall be satisfied at last. And who will not envy them the consolation of tears His hand shall wipe away!

What is required of the mourners of to-day that they may deserve this To-morrow? That they "be not sorrowful, even as others who have no hope."[2] That they say now in submission and in trust: "The Lord gave and the Lord hath taken away, blessed be the name of the Lord."[3]

All, all, had come by the King's highway, the way of the holy Cross. There is no other way to that Kingdom. Surely the King Himself should not have travelled by that road? Yet He upbraided His disciples who would have had Him go by another: "Ought not Christ to have suffered these things and so enter into His glory?"[4]

"Out of great tribulation." If we could only realise this lesson of the Cross as he did who saw that multitude and heard those words! He wrote them as he was bidden by our Lord Himself, "to the seven churches which are in Asia," signing himself "I, John, your brother and your partner *in tribulation and in the Kingdom.*"[5] See how he links the two.

Truly, "blessed is he that readeth and heareth the words of this prophecy, and keepeth those things which are written in it."[6] We can hardly read and ponder the blessed words of Scripture without drinking in their spirit and their strength.

---

1   Apoc. vii. 13-17.
2   I Thess. iv. 12.
3   Job i. 21.
4   S. Luke xxiv. 26.
5   Apoc. i. 9.
6   Apoc. i. 3.

For what things soever were written, were written for our learning," says St. Paul, "that through patience and the comfort of the Scriptures we might have hope."[1]

To whom, then, will Christ look at His coming for the welcome He surely deserves at our hands? To those whose lives have been marked with the saving sign of His Cross; who have borne its discipline uncomplainingly at least, maybe joyfully, in the end, like Simon the Cyrenean. To those in whom it has worked out that likeness to Himself which St. John tells us all that great multitude will bear. "It hath not yet appeared what we shall be. We know that when He shall appear, we shall be like Him."[2] To these He promises joy in His Second Coming: "You now indeed have sorrow, but I will see you again, and your heart shall rejoice, and your joy no man shall take from you." I see you now, and it is to bring you My Cross. But I will see you again to bring you reward beyond all your heart can desire. Shall not these cross-bearers "love His Coming," with St. Paul? "As to the rest, there is laid up for me a crown of justice, which the Lord, the just judge, will render to me in that day, and not only to me, but to them also that love His coming."[3] When men are "withering away for fear of what shall come upon the whole world," these are to be glad. "When these things begin to come to pass, look up, and lift up your heads, because your redemption is at hand."

"Look up!" What a sight will that be—the upturned faces of that multitude which no man can number—watching, waiting for the Face of their Redeemer. They have risen from the dead. Their bodies, resplendent with immortal beauty, have been restored to them in the integrity and perfection of the Resurrection; endowed with the gifts of glory, immortality, impassibility, agility, clarity. They can neither die nor suffer

---

1   Rom. xv. 4.
2   I John iii. 2.
3   II Tim. iv. 8.

any more; they can traverse space with the rapidity of light; they shine like the sun. But these new-found gifts and joys are forgotten in that eager, expectant gaze into the heavens. How they hail the Sign of the Son of Man, as, borne by Angels, it comes forth! How its glory is reflected on the brow and in the eyes of each and all! How impatiently they await Him whom it heralds! They are to see Him at last according to the promise: "Every eye shall see Him."[1] "My eyes shall see the King in His beauty,"[2] each heart is saying to itself: "Whom I myself shall see, and my eyes shall behold and not another."[3]

Think of that meeting of the Redeemer with His Redeemed! Of their joy in His glory, of His joy in them and in the reward He brings them—compensation, in measure heaped up and running over, for all they have lost for His sake. These are the mourners to be comforted—fathers, mothers, sons, come out of the tribulation of the Great War, who having done the Will of God as it is done on earth, in sacrifice, in anguish, in patience, and hope, are now to do it, according to their daily prayer, in everlasting joy and thankfulness, "as it is done in Heaven."

To wait, and work, and suffer for that Day—is it not worth while? "And so much the more as you see the day approaching,"[4] says St. Paul. "Watch!" is Our Lord's own injunction to His disciples: "Blessed are those servants whom their Lord when He cometh shall find watching."[5] "Watch ye, therefore, because you know not at what hour your Lord will come, at even, or at midnight, or at cock-crowing. Lest coming on a sudden He find you sleeping. And what I say to you I say to all. Watch!"[6]

What is it to watch? To be intent; to be alert; to stand at

1   Apoc. i. 7.
2   Isaias xxxiii. 17.
3   Job xix. 27.
4   Heb. x. 25.
5   S. Luke xii. 37.
6   S. Mark xiii. 35-37.

"attention." So to serve passing needs, as not to miss the one thing necessary. Not to be getting ready, but to be ready, with everything prepared. To note the signs of the times. To take precautions against surprise, against the weariness of waiting, against the languor of sloth, against the scoffing of those who ask in derision: "Where are the signs of His coming?" against the solicitations of those who say: "The time of our life is short and tedious...and after this we shall be as if we had not been... Come, therefore, and let us enjoy the good things that are present...Let us fill ourselves with costly wine and ointments... let us crown ourselves with roses before they be withered: let no meadow escape our riot. Let none of us go without his part in luxury: let us everywhere leave tokens of joy."[1]

Material things are absorbing, and bid fair to absorb still more the interest and the energies of men. We must give heed to our Lord's word of warning: "Watch!"

Watching was the attitude of the first Christians. The belief which prevailed so long that the Second Coming of Christ was near at hand must have been a powerful support during the three centuries of persecution when life was hard indeed and the way to heaven rough. The thought that "at even, or at midnight, or at cock-crowing" their Lord might come, would nerve His servants for a death of torture or for the perils of a hunted life. It would be compensation in the loss of friends and all things here below. And it would make them fervent in His service, for He had said: "Behold, I come quickly, and my reward is with Me to render to every man according to his works."[2]

The same expectation of Christ's speedy coming with His reward will be the consolation of mourners now. So short and so trivial, compared with the recompense prepared for it, is

---

1   Wisd. ii. 1, 2, 6-9.
2   Apoc. xxii. 12.

all suffering here, that St. Paul calls it "momentary and light."[1]
And St. Peter says: "You shall greatly rejoice if now you must
be for a little while made sorrowful in divers temptations, that
the trial of your faith (much more precious than gold which
is tried by the fire) may be found unto praise and glory and
honour at the appearing of Jesus Christ."[2]

1   II Cor. iv. 17.
2   I Peter i. 6-7.

THE FIRST SORROW

by William Adolphe Bouguereau

III
CHEERFUL GIVERS

I will not offer to the Lord my God
holocausts which cost me nothing.—II. Kings xxiv. 24.

MANY episodes of the crisis through which we are passing would mark an epoch at any less eventful time. But in this conflict, the most tremendous in history, they pass almost unnoticed. Revolutions, the downfall of dynasties, atrocities, victories, catastrophes by land and sea and air, new and startling achievements of science, succeed one another with a rapidity which at last stuns and stupefies. Nothing surprises us now, though we live with every nerve on tension. Individual, social, and national life are in a state of upheaval. Old standards no longer serve. We count our resources, in men as in money, in millions. England, forsaking her proud tradition, has turned herself into a camp and a munition factory, and nothing matters so long as the masses of men in khaki are equal to the demand, and so long as there is no pause in the steady output of guns and shells for the front.

Looking back upon two years of war, we may well be thankful and hopeful. The men and the munitions, the guns and the equipment which ought to have been ready when war was declared, are ready now. The whole country is roused at last and ready for any effort and any sacrifice necessary to ensure a decisive victory and a lasting peace. Four millions of our youth, of their own accord trained to arms and disciplined, have offered their all to secure it. And women are not behind men in devotion and self-sacrifice. In France they are doing the work, or nearly all the work, done by men. In England they have taken up farm labour, agricultural and munition work to release men for the front. And, what is more, women are showing the endurance as well as the daring of patriotism. In France men are followed to the station by their wives and children, walking by the side of the column, the same heroic spirit in all. With us, the partings are sad when the troop trains leave, but "every man goes off brave and confident, and almost every woman keeps back her tears till her man is out of sight."

And then?

And then not only must the home fires be kept burning, but courage and cheerfulness must be kept up also. It is hard, for day after day anxious eyes are scanning the lists of casualties, and the day-long and night-long strain on fortitude must be extreme. Life and labour have to go on as usual. That "men must work and women must weep" is not the lesson of this War. It has a loftier teaching—that in prayer and in work for others the courage of sacrifice must be found. But mothers are not wanting in generosity. Where the young lead the van, they are following. Our boys, hardly home from school, are teaching us lessons of devotion to duty, self-sacrifice, and trust in God which are simply magnificent. Many are leading their elders to victory on the field; all are nerving to a noble generosity their fathers and mothers at home. Yet the letters to and from home show that heroism is fairly divided between the dear lads and those they leave behind. Brave mothers are worthy of their boys, whose last letters will live in our memories among the beautiful things of the Great War. "Many a woman has been made a widow and childless, but if the joy and crown of her life were restored to her here, she would again send him forth to fulfil his high calling and vocation."[1] An officer says: "I have

---

1   Lady Frances Balfour.

written to many mothers and to many wives of mutilated men, and I reverence mothers beyond all womankind because of the replies I have received."

A young officer who fell on the field of honour wrote to his parents on June 30th, 1916, the day before the beginning of the British offensive:

"I am writing to you just before going into action to-morrow morning about dawn. I never felt more confident or cheerful in my life before. My idea in writing this letter is in case I am one of the 'costs' and get killed. I do not expect to be, but such things have happened and are always possible... It is impossible to fear death out here where one is no longer an individual but a member of a regiment and of an army. To be killed means nothing to me, and it is only you who suffer for it; you really pay the cost. I have been looking at the stars and thinking what an immense distance they are away. What an insignificant thing the loss of, say, forty years of life is compared with them. It seems scarcely worth talking about. Well, good-bye, you darlings. Try not to worry about it, and remember that we shall meet again really quite soon. This letter is going to be posted if...Lots of love. From your loving son."

The last words of an adjutant, struck down by a bullet in the forehead, were "Maman, France, Dieu." Thus did he sum up all his thoughts and all the love of his heart.

"Even the most ordinary youths seems suddenly to develop into full-grown heroes under the stress of battle." A boy killed in action on September 13th, 1916, in a letter written to his uncle a day or two before his death, declared that he wished for nothing but the accomplishment of God's will, whatever that might be; just that and nothing more: "I know that you never forget to pray for me, that I may always do the right thing. I keep myself in readiness to go. One never knows what moment the summons may come...I do not ask to be spared, but only that I may do my duty. Please pray for that one intention."

What consolation there is here for parents who at the cost of much self-sacrifice had prepared a noble career for their sons! God has outstripped their desires. His own were as far ahead of theirs as Heaven is above the earth. "A grand cause voluntarily espoused, with the knowledge that in fighting for King and Country they are serving their God in the highest possible way"[1]—what career could they have chosen equal to this? "Greater love than this no man hath, that a man lay

1   Cardinal Bourne.

down his life for his friends." It is the proof by which our Lord measured His own love. And He has deigned to ask the same proof at their hands. What must be the affection of the Heart of Jesus for those who have shown themselves capable of following His example here, of laying down with life all that it holds dear and precious, and just when it is opening out before them with all its possibilities and attractions, and with the high hopes and plans that youth and talent and courage inspire!

Do not say that this beautiful natural growth, unless vivified by a supernatural motive, is valueless for eternity. Say, rather, that the Author of nature and of grace, having given the lesser, will not withhold the greater gift; that He who uses nature for a foundation will infuse into these generous offerings, and to an extent beyond all expectation, the supernatural virtue which will make them acceptable in His sight. Those who make friends with our men in the hospitals know that in the vast majority of cases duty was the motive that led them to enlist: "I felt I ought to go," they say. And duty means what is due to conscience and to God. There must, of course, be the state of grace. A man must be in friendship with God: "If I should deliver my body to be burned and have not charity, it profiteth me nothing."[1] A Catholic prepares himself by the Sacraments before going to the front, and whilst in the state of grace, renews many times, at least indirectly, the offering of his life to God. Non-Catholics who are in good faith (i.e., to whom the claims of the Catholic Church on their obedience have never appealed as binding in conscience) may make their peace with God by a hearty act of contrition: "My God, I am sorry for all my sins because Thou art so good." May we not believe that, in reward for the generous offering of their lives, God gives the grace of true contrition to untold multitudes upon the battlefield, He who only waits for a thought or a sigh, to efface sins and to receive into His

---

1 I Cor. xiii. 3.

arms the soul that turns to Him? We may even hope that this supreme proof of love may have a merit to be compared with that of martyrdom, and a corresponding reward. Can the most ambitious love for those dear to us desire more for them than this? Let us encourage those who are going to the front, by the thought of the merit which the offering of their life, made in a state of grace, has before God. God knows they need courage. And this supernatural foundation for it will secure it far more effectually than the mistaken kindness of refusing to consider the possibility of their being among the "costs."

And for ourselves let us bear in mind that in our present suffering we have abundant material for future glory and joy. With our dear ones we have made the sacrifice of career, and home, and comfort. Their privations and pains are felt at home as keenly as in camp, or trench, or prison abroad. Wives and mothers have a claim upon God which their generosity gives them. If it be His Will to accept the life that has been offered for His cause, in the service of King and country, those who share in that sacrifice will have part in the reward by and by. In many homes there will be distress, keener, perhaps, than death, when our armies come back from the trenches. But we need not, we should not, forecast. God will be there with His grace whatever comes; we may safely leave in His hands the results to those we love when this terrible conflict is closed at last.

THE SERMON ON THE MOUNT

from an Altarpiece by Henrik Olrik
St. Matthew's Church, Copenhagen

IV

"BLESSED ARE THEY THAT MOURN"

THE Twelve must have been startled. It was teaching at variance with the whole bent of the Jewish mind. Accustomed to ask their Master in private for the explanation of what they had not understood in His instruction to the crowd, they may well have said to Him on the way down from the Mount: "Lord, why are they blessed that mourn?"

And He would have begun to prepare their minds for the mystery of the Cross, saying, perhaps, what He said at the Last Supper: "I have many things to say to you, but you cannot bear them now."[1] There was no subject harder to bring home to them than the value of the Cross. Up to the very hour of His Ascension, their questions showed how little the truth had penetrated their understanding, above all how scandalised and pained they were that pain should be in store *for Him*. It needed the coming of the Holy Spirit, who was to teach them all things, to enlighten them practically on this point, and make them soon after, when they had been beaten with rods, "go from the presence of the council rejoicing that they were accounted worthy to suffer for the name of Jesus."[2] From that time forward there was nothing they taught with more persistence, nothing they had more at heart to impress upon their converts, than "that through many tribulations we must

1   S. John xvi. 12.
2   Acts v. 41.

enter into the kingdom of God."[1]

We must suffer because we have sinned, and it is due to the Justice of God that we should be punished here or hereafter. When chastisement comes to us, either directly from God, or through the ministry of others, it provides us with the opportunity of paying here, where a relatively small atonement is accepted in discharge of our debt, what will otherwise be exacted to the last farthing in the life to come. Are not the mourners blessed who accept their chastisement from the hand of God with humility, and bear it with patience?

And mourners are blessed, because in this life pain and sorrow are never purely chastisement. If suffered in a Christian spirit and in a state of grace, they merit for us further grace, and the glory which in Heaven corresponds to grace: "For that which is at present momentary and light of our tribulation worketh for us above measure exceedingly an eternal weight of glory."[2]

Once more, they are blessed that mourn, because union with God, which is our happiness here and hereafter, can only be reached by the road of detachment and suffering, by "the King's highway of the holy Cross." "To some," says à Kempis, "this seems a hard saying." Even so, we must accept the consequences of our position. We are not only exiles and sinners, but God's children, aye, and "most dear children,"[3] yet making our way home to Him through difficulties and dangers on every side, through good fortune and bad, the daily worries of life, and those crucial hours when the sword of anguish rends the very soul asunder.

What force can bear us safely through tests so many and so various? One only—our faith. "Sola fides sufficit," the Church sings triumphantly all along her course. Yes, faith

1   Acts xix. 21.
2   II Cor. iv. 17.
3   Ephes. v. 1.

alone suffices, but it does suffice. We may lean with our whole weight upon it in the heaviest trials and it will bear the pressure. Martyrs, confessors, sufferers of every age, have proved it; the mourners of our own day in the agony through which all are passing are proving it by a heroism which is the admiration of heaven and earth.

The faith of our baptism is in us all. But it must be stirred if it is to give out its fragrance and its force. It is stirred by prayer, which brings the omnipotent grace of God to our aid. It is stirred by our own effort to co-operate with His grace, by the resignation which says, even with difficulty and tears: "Father, not my will, but Thine be done!"

There is not so far to go from the effort of faith, which is resignation, to the effort which is heroism. For God is magnanimous in His dealings with us. He asks a little in order to give much. The trials He sends for our good, bear with them, not their grace only, but their recompense. We gaze with amazement at the achievements of God's servants in the way of sacrifice, but what we do not see is that "underneath are the everlasting arms."[1]

Faith is regarded by unbelievers in one of two ways. Some look upon it as a slavery to which by the sacrifice of our reason we have committed ourselves, and they pity, or affect to pity, the children of the Church. Others, applying the test that the tree is known by its fruits, frankly confess, as they watch a servant of God under trial: "I wish I could believe like that." They recognise in faith a faculty of which they are deprived. Would that they could go on to recognise the part that the will has to play in the submission of the understanding to "the obedience of faith,"[2] and that they would win by prayer the humility of heart, which would procure for them what excites their envy!

But we also, the children of the Church, are too often in fault

1   Deut. xxxiii. 27.
2   Rom. xvi. 26.

here. We know that the faith of our baptism is a gift beyond all price, containing in itself the germ of all other gifts. But we do not consider that as a germ it needs tending if it is to develop and grow to maturity, and that in proportion to the care we bestow upon it will be its fruits in our life here and in our eternity hereafter. The Saints of God are those whose cultivated faith produces mature fruits. This it is that makes them quick to see His chastisement of sin in public and private sorrows, and so ready to humble themselves before Him. So ready, too—and this is harder—to see His love in chastisement; not to lose confidence under it; not to let it estrange them from Him. Trial, so far from provoking such estrangement, should drive us into His arms. When our best and dearest are there, where else shall we go to find them?

This world is not our home, and those who try to make it such lose sight of the true Home and fail to reach it. Hence, the reminders of exile on every side. Blessed are they who take them as reminders, who hold the good things of life with a loose hand and see them go without despair. We are not required to be callous. The tender heart of St. Paul viewed with horror a characteristic of "the last days, when men shall be... ungrateful, unmerciful, without kindness...without affection."[1] There is no more touching scene in the Acts of the Apostles than his farewell to the faithful of Ephesus who were to see his face no more.[2] He who "gloried in tribulation"[3] was gentle and patient with the tempted and the troubled, rejoicing with them that rejoiced, weeping with them that wept,[4] glorying, above all, in their patience and faith. He has a whole litany of the achievements of faith and patience combined, and among these we find: "Women received their dead raised to life again."[5]

---

1   II. Tim. iii. 2,3.
2   Acts xx. 37, 38.
3   Rom. v. 3.
4   Rom. xii. 15.
5   II Thess. i. 4.

Had we sat with the Twelve at the feet of Christ on the Mount of the Beatitudes and heard Him give those wonderful blessings to His followers; had we seen the earnestness of His countenance as He said: "Blessed are they that mourn," would not His words, followed up by His example and by the glory of His Resurrection, have come back to us in after years to strengthen us for our own conflict and tribulation?

DAVID MOURNS THE DEATH OF ABSALOM

by Gustave Doré

V
UNCOVENANTED MERCIES

BUT there is a class of mourners whose very faith and love of God is a source of added pain. They would bear willingly to the end of life the loneliness in which the loss of one they love has left them, if only they had the assurance that he who has been called away was ready. The keenest part of their trouble is that they do not find in the past sufficient warrant for this assurance, and there is no one to tell how the end came and the dispositions in which it found him.

Yet even this supreme trial is not too severe for the Faith and Hope that cry still: "I know in Whom I have believed, and I am certain that He is able to keep that which I have committed to Him."[1] I believe in His promise: "Ask and it shall be given you.. for every one that asketh receiveth."[2] "Although He should slay me, I will trust in Him."[3]

There is much comfort to be found in the remembrance that to God there is no past nor future. All is present. You prayed, perhaps, for years. Yet, when the last moment came, there was nothing to tell that your prayer was heard. You are praying still—but too late you say, since all is over. No, it is not too late; it is never too late. Before the end came, God saw all your prayers to come. And He has promised: "Ask and you shall

---

1   II. Tim. i. 12.
2   S. Matt. vii. 7, 8.
3   Job xiii. 15.

receive." It may be urged that where others are concerned, this promise is conditional, since God, though He gives grace, will never force the free will of man. But it is also true that it is always in His power to give efficacious grace, that is, grace so powerful that He knows it will have its effect. Are not these— God's uncovenanted mercies—the "great mercies" for which David prays: "Have mercy on me, O God, according to Thy great mercy"?[1]

Do not say: "I have no right to count on such efficacious grace." If right were our only plea, we might well despair! But it is our need, our misery that is our right.

And do not say: "Such graces are beyond the power of my weak prayer to obtain." The promise is to prayer, however weak, to persevering prayer, however unworthy: "The prayer of him that humbleth himself shall pierce the clouds and shall not depart till the Most High behold."[2]

If the Saints were among the wary ones here, I might well despond; I might think my hope presumptuous. But it is in God's servants that hope is boldest: "who against hope believe in hope"[3]; who tell me I can never hope too much from the mercy of God, for His "tender mercies are over all His works."[4]

"Know ye that no one hath hoped in the Lord and hath been confounded."[5]

"Who hath called on Him and He despised him?"[6]

"He gave them their desire: they were not defrauded of that which they craved."[7]

"Thou shalt know that the Lord Thy God is a strong and faithful God."[8]

---

1   Ps. l. 3.
2   Ecclus. xxxv. 21.
3   Rom. iv. 18.
4   Ps. cxliv. 9.
5   Ecclus. ii. 11.
6   Ecclus. ii. 12.
7   Ps. lxxvii. 29, 30.
8   Deut. vii. 9.

"He is not a man that He should repent."[1]

"In my distress I will call upon the Lord and I will cry to my God."[2]

"Help me who have no other helper but Thee, O Lord."[3]

"Let them trust in Thee who know Thee, O Lord."[4]

"Trust Him, He cannot stand proof against your trust," says another faithful soul.

"Lord, I count upon You without knowing how...but I count upon You."[5]

But what need have I of the assurance of the Saints, when I have the solemn and unqualified promises of our Lord Himself, urged upon us by every one of the Evangelists:

"If you being evil know how to give good gifts to your children, how much more will your Father who is in heaven give good things to them that ask Him."[6]

"I say unto you, all things whatsoever you ask when you pray, believe that you shall receive, and they shall come unto you."[7]

"I say to you, ask and it shall be given you: seek and you shall find: knock, and it shall be opened to you. For everyone that asketh receiveth; and he that seeketh findeth; and to him that knocketh, it shall be opened."[8]

"Amen, amen, I say to you: if you ask the Father anything in My name, He will give it you...Ask, and you shall receive, that your joy may be full."[9]

What shall compel Him if not my trust in His promises, my trust in Himself? "I know in whom I have believed and I am

1 I Kings xv. 29.
2 II Kings xxii. 7.
3 Esther xiv. 14.
4 Gradual for Septuagesima Sunday.
5 Venerable Mere de Sales Chappuis.
6 S. Matth. vii. 11.
7 S. Mark xi. 24.
8 S. Luke xi. 9, 10.
9 S. John xvi. 23, 24.

certain that He is able to keep that which I have committed to Him against that day."

I know—for is He not "the Lord God, merciful and gracious, of much compassion and true?"

I am certain—for He has said: "Delight in the Lord and He will give thee the requests of thy heart."

He is able—for He is "the Almighty God, the Most High."

To keep that which I have committed unto Him—oh, how often and with such trust in His fidelity!

Against that day—the day when He will show me my trust has not been in vain, the day when He will give me the request of my heart.

> I waited for the Lord a little space.
>   So little! in whose sight as yesterday
> Passes a thousand years:—I cried for grace,
>   Impatient of delay.
>
> He waited for me—ah so long! For He
>   Sees in one single day a loss or gain
> That bears a fruit through all eternity:—
>   My soul, did He complain?
>
> *Patience.*—R. H. Benson.

VI
SOME MORE VALIANT ONES

THERE are moments, perhaps, in the lives of all of us when we have felt as if we—yes, *even we*—could be capable of great things should the opportunity offer, and motive and strength be sufficient to brace us to the effort. We read of the deeds of men and women in days of persecution, in the French Revolution, in times of war, and our hearts glow with enthusiasm. This is not altogether unprofitable sentiment. We are probably too well taught by experience to base any hopes of ourselves in critical occasions on our own strength. But our belief that with the test comes the grace equal to it gives us confidence, and we almost desire the test and the grace that would be victorious in our weakness.

If this be so our chance has come. The days now upon us are days of persecution, days of revolution and of war, which have unchained passions fiercer than history has ever witnessed, and call for sacrifice which would have wrung all joy out of life could it have been foreseen. But with the need and the call for heroism has come the strength. The Christianity of the world, and the civilisation Christianity has given to the world, the freedom, the homes, the lives, that Christianity has sanctified—all this is at stake.

As late as the summer of 1914 there were people in England still willing to believe the country had nothing to fear from the powerful neighbour who for forty years had been preparing his attack. Then came that eventful autumn with its call to arms. "Your King and country want you!" put an end to illusion and brought home the nation's peril to every man and woman in the land. Eighteen months later those words had raised by voluntary enlistment an army of over 5,000,000 men, an effort, the King told his people,[1] far surpassing that of any other nation in similar circumstances recorded in history. The world was taken by surprise. The enemy was dumbfounded. In the thoroughness of his preparation for this war, two possible assets on the other side had been overlooked—Providence and Patriotism. And these have sufficed for us. In the justice of our cause is our strength. This war is not only a crusade, but the greatest of crusades. It may result in the restoration to Christendom of the Holy Places for which during two centuries our forefathers shed their blood. But its immediate objective is something wider and more vital. It is to free, not Palestine alone, nor Europe alone, but the whole world from the curse of German militarism, from the deluge of evils which in the name of Material Progress, High Civilisation, "Kultur," is threatening the earth.

We are fighting, not only for our own safety, for the rights of other nations, for the independence of the smaller peoples of Europe, but for the preservation of those Christian principles which created the civilisation of the world. Never have those principles been so shamelessly ignored. Never were the Holy Places polluted by infidels or by barbarians as the sacred and venerable shrines of Europe are to-day by Christian hands. Never have outrages against women and children, prisoners and priests, been more cowardly and revolting. We are struggling with a "culture" which would reduce the world to a state of savagery and oppression, materialism, and irreligion without parallel in

---

1   May 25, 1916.

history. What wonder the conflict inspires with heroism all who have the interests of religion and humanity at heart!

No price is too great for the victory we must win. All must help by service and by sacrifice. Whilst millions of men raised in a few months are fighting like veterans, women and girls at home are taking up new duties, replacing skilled men in the work of providing munitions of war and equipment for the forces, and maintaining the trade of the country. In this unfamiliar and arduous work they are showing extraordinary adaptability and efficiency. Not only in the work of tending the sick and caring for the wounded and bereaved as in other wars have they to bestir themselves to-day: "To look after the welfare of the whole nation in its economic, social, and national phases is the duty of women during the war and afterwards."[1] "By universal consent," says Sir William Robertson, "the women have done great work in this war, and shown splendid fortitude in times of anxiety, sorrow, and bereavement."

The War Office pays a similar tribute:—

"Since the outbreak of war the women of Britain have shown themselves ready and anxious to undertake every form of work where their services could be accepted...have shown themselves capable of successfully replacing the stronger sex in practically every calling...Employers readily admit that the results achieved by the temporary employment of women far exceed their original estimates...Wives have taken up their husbands' work, sisters their brothers', daughters their fathers', even mothers their sons'...Untiring efforts must be devoted to amplify and extend the scope of women's usefulness, by which alone our country can hope to emerge victorious from a struggle without parallel in her long and glorious history."

But the spirit of self-sacrifice thus shown in so many and such various departments of activity is far from being woman's

1   Speech of Mr. W. M. Hughes, Prime Minister of Australia, to the Women of England.

highest achievement at this time of stress and sorrow. Patriotism can do much. The resolution of the women of France, now leading the teams, that their men when they return to them shall not find a field nor a garden fallow, is admirable. But it is not in physical effort or in the promptings of merely natural patriotism that truest greatness is found. We get dazed by the magnificence of the self-sacrifice by sea and land and air that our daily papers set before us. But there are deeds they cannot tell. There are battlefields in millions of quiet homes far away. We are paying a price for victory such as we never paid before. If the efficiency of our new armies has filled the world with admiration or consternation, and the steadfastness of the men at sea has never been surpassed, the sacrifice of the dead and the stricken has never been equalled, nor has mourning throughout the land ever been so general or so deep. Every day the front sends home its heavy toll of casualties. Our churches are filled with congregations of mourners. Scarcely a home or a heart is without its agony of desolation or of suspense.

God is taking at its word many a soul that had desired to do great things for Him. Are we ready for this?

> Nearer, my God, to Thee, nearer to Thee,
> E'en though a cross it be that raises me!

How many say or sing these words without realising their import and without the faintest wish that their prayer should be heard! For it is a prayer, and one that bears testimony to the deep conviction of the human heart that of all God's levers suffering is the most powerful, that it is by the Cross and contact with Jesus Crucified that He has lifted many an ordinary soul to the heights where He awaited it.

In some stirring words to men in camp on Salisbury Plain, Cardinal Bourne exhorted them to make full use of their splendid material sacrifices. May not those who are so closely associated with these sacrifices take home to themselves the

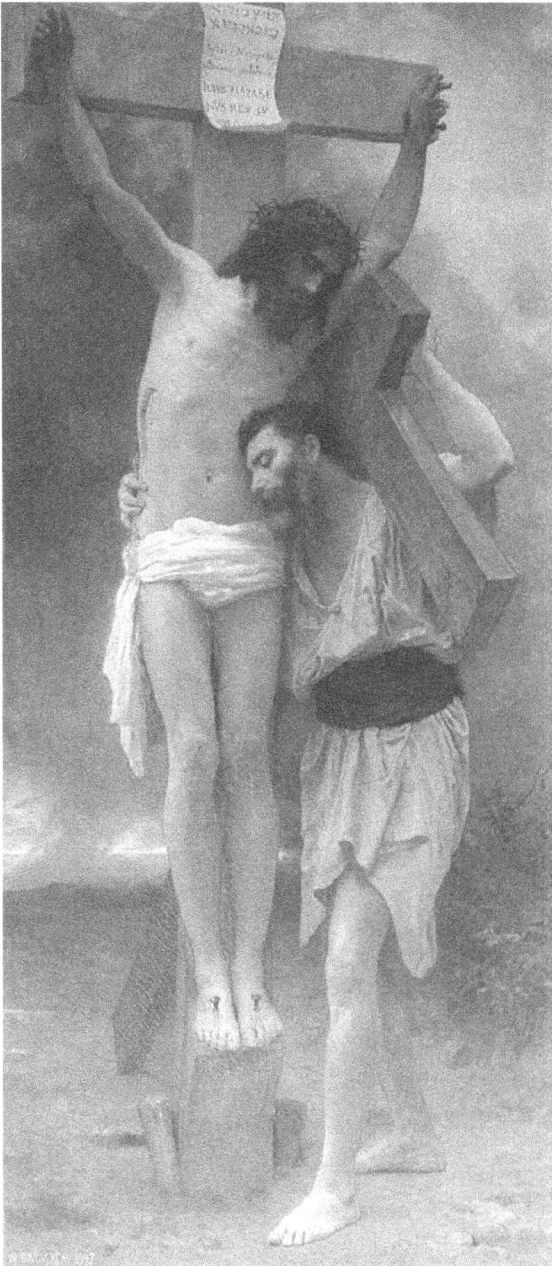

COMPASSION!

by William Adolphe Bouguereau

same exhortation? Because this is a time of severe demand upon us, it is also a season of quite exceptional grace. It is God's way always to meet need by supply—enough grace to meet any demand upon it, superabundant grace where it is asked for. Times of national mourning like the present, periods of acute personal trial, are thus epochs of Divine visitation. When the crisis is over, people wonder at the force which bore them through.

We may meet what is called a crushing trial by just sufficient resignation to the Will of God to avoid sin, but with an amount of morbid self-pity fatal to anything like heroism. Or, when the first pang of grief has passed, the heart may lift itself up to God in its agony, and the will adhere firmly to Him through conflict, prostration, desolation. The grace is there to help effort, but the will must make the effort. How often has a soul, struck down by what is termed a crushing blow, refused to be crushed, and, co-operating with grace, been lifted once for all from the low-lying plain of mediocrity, where it seemed destined to remain for ever, into a region where pain, so far from alienating the soul from God, draws it very near to Him; so far from driving out peace, strengthens its hold; to a Mount where the mourner stands beside the Mother of Sorrows, whose soul magnified the Lord on Calvary as peacefully and as loyally as when Elizabeth's congratulations drew forth her first glorious song of praise.

A great cross nobly borne will free a soul from selfishness and miseries that held it fast for well-nigh a lifetime. It will bring mature holiness by a quick growth. The affections that have been wrenched and torn from the creature have flung themselves upon the Creator, and in Him have found again in fuller measure and with firmer grasp what they had lost. The love of God that once burned low and feebly, fed by the wood of the Cross, has become a consuming fire, a force that carries all before it.

See the world to-day! In the hearts of fathers and mothers, of wives and of sisters, is an anguish and a grandeur of sacrifice, the depth and merit of which are known to God alone. It called forth at first the affectionate or the respectful sympathy of those who in different degrees shared it, true sympathy that did what it could and that can do so little—how little only the poor mourners who gratefully acknowledge it know. Then, when the stupor of the blow had passed and full consciousness returned, the silent agony began, unshared, because of the rapidity with which fresh claims are pressing; unshared, too, because in their generosity the bereaved ones feign an outward brightness lest their cloud should overshadow the lives of others. Friends see them and are consoled. "Time," they say, "is doing its healing work." How little they know!

Oh, will not the fathers and the mothers, the wives, the fiancees, the sisters of this awful time be counted by God among the victims who have served to appease His anger for the sins of men and to save a guilty world! Has there not been an out-pouring of grace on old and young alike, to present a sacrifice, the grandeur of which has no counterpart in history? Here and there the veil is lifted to show us deeds and deaths as generous as ever earth has seen, samples of what we shall know when the men come home from the trenches, but to be fully known only when the secrets of all hearts shall be revealed. Then, too, shall we learn of the silent heroism of millions whose names have no place in history, but in the Book of Life, as we may well believe, are among the most famous there.

The Sacrifice--For Humanity's Sake

by Louis Raemaekers

VII
RACHEL

"Pity the countless mothers in anguish for the fate of their sons."

IT is the mothers to whom our hearts go out in deepest sympathy. And in gratitude. As the Catholic instinct is to fly to the Altar for refuge from the divine judgments, and to offer in atonement for our guilt the infinite merits of Him who is "always living to make intercession for us,"[1] so may we humbly add to this offering of infinite worth the sacrifice of the mothers of Christendom to-day.[2] "Look upon the Face of Thy Christ,"[3] we say, as the Sacred Host is elevated at the Consecration. "Pity the mothers," we may add, "who are uniting their sacrifice with His." Our Lord remembers that on Calvary His Mother's offering went up to the Father with His own. Will not that remembrance move Him to welcome all companionship in suffering and in atonement?

"There stood by the Cross of Jesus His Mother."[4] Many mothers are called to share her agony now. Where will they

---

1 Heb. vii. 25.
2 Among the cartoons in which Raemaekers has memorialised the thought of the day is "The Sacrifice." It appeared at Christmastide, 1915, and represents the Mother of God holding in her arms the Divine Infant, while round her gather the mothers of Christendom with their infant sons, whom they, too have been called on to surrender for the sake of mankind. It touched the thought of the hour in a manner no words could do and solaced many Christian mothers, who on a sad Christmas Day were mourning the loss of their sons.—*Land and Water.*
3 Ps. lxxxiii. 10.
4 S. John xix. 25.

endure with greater fortitude than by Mary's side, with her example to teach and strengthen them? She was on Calvary because Her Son had need of her there. She was to be His last gift to His followers, to John and to us all. He gave her as a Mother, to care for us, to compassionate us, to feel for us with the sympathy of one who has suffered as no other excepting only Himself. "When Jesus, therefore, had seen His Mother and the disciple standing whom He loved, He saith to His Mother: "Woman, beheld thy son!" After that He saith to the disciple: "Behold thy Mother." He gave her as a mourner for the consolation of mourners. As the wounded turn instinctively for sympathy to Him who was "wounded for our iniquities and bruised for our sins,"[1] so should mourners look—to Him first who says, "Learn of Me," but with Him, and as He bids us, to the Mother of Sorrows beneath the Cross.

> Sorrow with Sorrow loves to dwell,
> Mourners their tale to mourners tell,
> Who loves the Cross should love thee well,
> My Mother![2]

The Catholic Church has always believed that in the person of St. John a world-wide family was confided to Mary from the Cross. Now, when God entrusts a mission to any one of His creatures, He gives to His ambassador, as credentials, the qualifications for its honourable discharge, and this in proportion to the importance of the embassy. Mary was to be the new Mother of the human race, "Mother of all the living" in a sense which Eve, who so sadly betrayed her motherhood, never merited. Mary, therefore, had given to her a sympathy with her suffering children, and compassion for their ignorance and mistakes and miseries, a comprehension of their difficulties and troubles, an indulgence for their weakness and waywardness, that fit her for such an office. She was to be Virgin

---

1   Isaias liii. 5.
2   F. Oakeley.

of Virgins, Virgin most venerable, Virgin most renowned, but, above all, Virgin most merciful, Virgin most faithful, Comfort of the afflicted.

What a resource to the mourning women of the world at this hour is the Mother beneath the Cross! "Look and do according to the pattern that was shown thee on the Mount,"[1] is said to them now. And many are heeding the injunction! Many stand beside her on Calvary to-day and are staying their breaking hearts on the broken but strong heart of the Mother of Sorrows. She is our teacher there. "Behold thy Mother," Christ says to each of us in sorrow. "Look and do according to the pattern shown thee on the Mount." Now, what was it that He noted in her, that St. John has left on record? One thing only—that she stood. She stood as the priest stands to sacrifice. She stood to see, to hear, to feel all. She stood—a mark for every gibe, for every insult flung at Him. She stood—as a follower of her Son, erect, intent, tranquil, resolute. The strain upon every fibre of that sensitive frame was intense and grew as the hours wore on. No relief by the suspension of consciousness; no dullness of agony; every sense and faculty at its keenest to the end. Yet she stood through those three hours, her outward bearing in perfect harmony with the steadfast soul within.

And her words? We hear of none. Her Son had been silent before His tormentors, so would she be. Every instinct of the most loyal of disciples, the most tender of mothers, was wounded by pitiless outrage. Yet there was no protest beyond the tears that told her agony. As her physical powers, so her spiritual faculties were taxed to the utmost, and they stood the test with absolute fidelity and perfection. There was no faltering of her faith, no relaxation of her fortitude, no wavering in her trust, no disturbance of her peace. She stood, says St. John: "There stood by the cross of Jesus His Mother." What need to say more!

---

1 Exod. xxv. 40.

"And from that hour the disciple took her to his own." Our Lord makes His dying gift to us, but it is for us to accept or to reject it. The disciple took her to his own. He took her in deepest gratitude from the hands and from the Heart of his Saviour; in filial gratitude to her who in that hour of bitter parting was asked to accept such an exchange-

There is a picture of the Crucifixion which draws attention to the compact between the Mother of Jesus and the disciple whom He loved. At His word they have drawn closer together and stand, the hands of John in Mary's, beneath the wounded feet. In that hour of her universal motherhood, solemnly given her on Calvary, each one of His disciples whom Jesus loves is entrusted to her. And she accepts the charge, and the compact is sealed in His Blood.

From that hour the disciple took her to his own. Not merely or mainly to the shelter of his roof, but to all that was his—to the veneration, the love, the gratitude, the trust that belong to her alone. He took her as his model, the pattern shown him on the Mount. Where John went, Mary went, to be to him through long years of apostolic labour, refreshment, counsel, and support. At Patmos he saw her clothed with the sun, the moon beneath her feet. But it was as the Mother of Sorrows he loved her best. Not in her dazzling glory, but in the darkness and amid the horrors of Calvary, standing, bruised and broken beneath the Cross, sharing the shame. Erect in her fortitude, grand in her desolation, steadfast in faith, and hope, and loving submission to the Father's Will, as in the hour when he took her to his own—such was the image of her in the heart of John to the end.

Mother, we, too, are thy children. John stood for us all on Calvary. We were given into thy care with him. He Who looked down on thee from the Cross was God. He saw through all time. He saw the Calvarys that were to come, and those who age after age were to stand beneath the Cross. If they are to be His true followers they must stand there with thee. The Divine Model shown on the Mount must be their Exemplar. But He will not be held aloft for their imitation without thee by his side. Beholding our Mother—so we climb up to Him. As it was for thee once, so is it for us now—darkness and desolation all around. Of all the Calvarys earth has seen, one only excepted, ours is the most awful. The world is one wide Golgotha. On every side women are mourning their dead. Make room for us, holy Mother, by thy side. Teach us to look up with thee to the great High-Priest and to unite our sacrifice with His. Get us some part of thy fortitude and generosity. Help us to thank God, even through our tears, that our dearest and our best have been counted worthy to offer to God the greatest proof of love. It is the cause of God that they have upheld. The Christianity of the world is at stake. To preserve it for the generations to come, they have laid down their lives. If a cup of cold water will have its reward, what will theirs be? The hour of reward will come, but not just yet. Help us to stand bravely by thy side till the darkness clears away and, in the light of the Resurrection, we who have mourned with thee shall rejoice, and our joy no man shall take from us.

The Raising of Lazarus

by Julius Schnorr von Carolsfeld

VIII
AT BETHANY
A LESSON IN TRUST

O UR Lord had three special friends at Bethany—a brother and two sisters. They were His friends to the end, which cannot be said of all who hung about Him, praised, and blessed Him. When trouble came to Him and other doors were closed against Him, their home was always ready with its reverent welcome and hospitality.

"Now, Jesus loved Martha, and her sister Mary and Lazarus." St. John is going to tell us of the trouble that came upon this favoured three.

Lazarus fell ill, and his sisters at once had recourse to their divine Friend. Their message showed their trust. There was no request that He would come quickly, as the sick man was already in extremity. "Lord, he whom Thou lovest is sick." That was all. They knew Him. What need was there for more? Whilst one watched by the pillow, the other sat at the window to tell of the first sign on the white road of His approach. The hours dragged on, and at length their messenger returned— but alone! They plied him with eager questions. Had he seen the Master? Was He far behind? Oh, it was hard to tell them! Yes, he had found the Master teaching, a great crowd about Him as usual. "The sickness was not unto death," He said. This was the only answer. There was no message to them, no sign of any intention to come to them. (It is here—a significant place—that St. John interrupts his narrative to tell us that "Jesus loved Martha, and her sister Mary, and Lazarus.") Think of their distress, and how it deepened as the end drew on.

Lazarus died, and the funeral rites followed quickly —the hired wailing of Eastern mourning; the burial; the coming of friends whose sympathy was not unmixed with surprise at the absence of One who had hitherto professed such regard for them. But He was of course unaware of the gravity of the illness, as His words, that the sickness was not unto death, proved.

The sisters heard all in silence as, barefoot and covered with their black veils, they sat on the ground, bewailing their dead. Every word was agony to them. They could not understand. His ways were "past finding out." Temptation whispered that He had failed them. But they fought the misgivings and the despondency always ready to assail those in sorrow, and clung to Him still in trust. What else was that cry of loving expostulation with which they threw themselves at His feet when He came at last: "Lord, if Thou hadst been here my brother had not died!" Martha added, wistfully: "But now also I know that whatsoever Thou wilt ask of God, God will give it Thee." Unwavering trust still; yet no petition, no attempt to bend the Will of God to hers. Mary, too, as was her wont, abandoned herself unreservedly to Him in silence and in hope. He saw their tears. He knew their hearts—that was enough.

The divine purpose in the resurrection of Lazarus, our Lord Himself tells us, was that the Son of God might be glorified. But it was also that those two faithful hearts might be rewarded when the Cross had done its work of sanctification there. What we have to learn from the sisters, standing on either side of the Master at the tomb, is resignation and trust. Had He been content to weep with them there and to lead them back again, strengthened by His grace to wait for His consolation till the Resurrection at the last Day, they would have made His Will their own. This is what He asks of our trust—to wait a little while "till He shall have fulfilled His will in us"[1] by the sanctification of the Cross.

"But the trust of Martha and Mary was rewarded immediately," it may be urged. "Lazarus was restored to them. Where conditions are so different it is unfair to expect the same result."

Yes, Lazarus was restored to them. And a little later Christ Himself was restored from the tomb to His weeping friends. But where would be the merit of faith and hope if reward was always to follow immediately upon trust? "Because thou hast seen Me, Thomas, thou hast believed," was our Lord's reproach to Thomas; "blessed are they that have not seen and have believed."[2]

1   Job xxiii. 14.
2   S. John xx. 29.

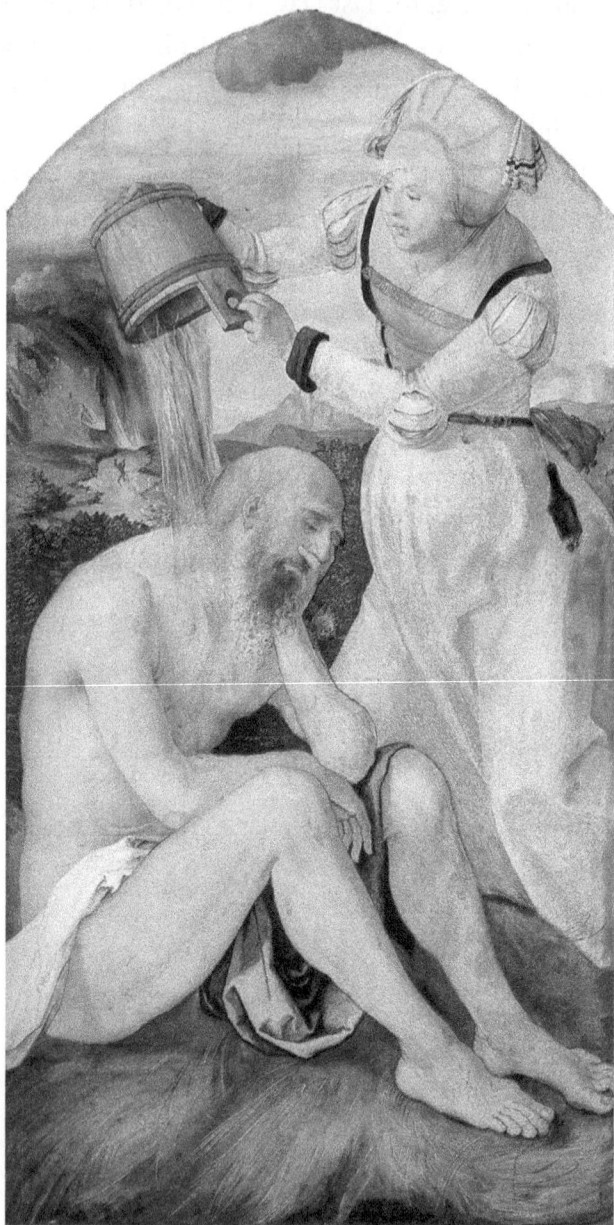

JOB AND HIS WIFE

by Albrecht Durer

IX
WHY WONDERFUL?

THOMAS À KEMPIS knows human nature well. Few things in it astonish him. He knows us well, and, on the whole, takes our weaknesses and inconsistencies with extraordinary equanimity. So that when we find him surprised, not to say indignant, we are startled to more than usual attention!

"It is wonderful," he says, speaking in the name of Christ, "it is wonderful that thou wilt not from the very bottom of thy heart commit thyself wholly to Me, with all things that thou canst desire to have."[1]

Why wonderful?

Because we ought to know our God better by this time. Mistrust should be an impossibility for us. The servants of God under the Old Law may have found it hard to cast themselves with all their care upon Him whom, after all, they knew very imperfectly, if we compare their knowledge with that vouchsafed to us since the Incarnation Yet where shall we find more absolute trust invited, enjoined, and expressed than in the history of the chosen people, and even outside it, as in the case of Job?

Why wonderful?

Because with our faith all right, our practice is all wrong, or at least woefully defective. We know that God loves and cares

---

1   The Imitation of Christ, Book iii. c. 27.

for us; that He can do all He wills for us; that He can never be mistaken in His plans for our real and lasting happiness, nor in the means He takes to carry them into effect. Because the lives of others and our own experience have taught us that He deserves the most absolute trust, the unquestioning surrender to Him of all we are, and have, and desire. Because He has never yet deceived nor failed us. Because in proportion—or, rather, out of all proportion—to our confidence has come His help to us in time of need. Because we are beginning at last to understand His ways; to learn that as children we must be content to tell Him of our wants, and then to wait His time and take His way of helping as the best for us.

Why wonderful?

Because of "the great cloud of witnesses"[1] above us, of the rejoicing family waiting for us at Home, of that "multitude which no man can number" who have reached the end of their trial and received the promised reward. They have gained the prize for which we are striving. They behold face to face what "we now see through a glass in a dark manner."[2] And what is their testimony to Him who "prepared all their ways"[3]? "Oh, trust Him, trust Him!" they cry out to us: He is the 'Faithful and True.'[4] "He hath done all things well."[5] "The Lord is faithful in all His words."[6] "Of all the words which the Lord promised to perform for us, not one hath failed."[7]

" 'He hath done all things well.' Not one of us now that thinks he was overtried, that God exacted too much, or was ever unmindful of him in time of trial. Men saw our trial but not our grace. 'If it had not been that the Lord was with us,'[8]

1 Heb. xii. 1.
2 I Cor. xiii. 12
3 Judith ix. 5.
4 Apoc. xix. 11.
5 S. Mark vii. 37.
6 Ps. cxliv. 13.
7 Josue xxiii. 14.
8 Ps. cxxiii. 1.

strength would have failed us utterly. But He *was* with us and we were able to do all things in Him who strengthened us. What he has done for us He will do for you. Trust Him, keep close to Him, cast all your care upon Him, for 'underneath are the everlasting arms.' [1]"

Why wonderful?

Because to hesitate is to mistrust either His wisdom or His love. It is more likely to be His love. We know that He *can* do the best for us. But *will* He? Or have we a lurking suspicion that His views, if certainly the best in the long run, are yet so infinitely above our own and demand such sacrifice of present hopes that we cannot bring ourselves to fall in with them? How foolish this is! We lament the shortsightedness that prefers the present to the future. Yet this is what we are always doing when we mistrust the will of God. Folded up in that will, as in a scroll, is the design of God for our happiness, planned from eternity. Each hour as it passes unrolls for us a portion of that scroll, bringing to light what has had eternal existence in the Mind of God, and been approved there or permitted for our good. In the events of each day, in the pain or pleasure of each moment, whether the destinies of empires are concerned, or the fabric of the simplest home-life—all has been written there by Him who doth all things well. May we not trust Him to have some interest in the execution of His own eternal designs? And can we do better than share that interest with Him, work with Him as far as may be for their furtherance—and leave the rest to Him?

The lesson of trust, taught by the blessed Mother of God to the waiters at the marriage feast of Cana: "Whatsoever He shall say to you, do ye," is left us by all those whom it has brought in safety to their journey's end. They teach it up to the gates of eternity, and, passing within the portals of their eternal home,

---

1   Deut. xxxiii. 27.

turn round to us, still amid the difficulties and perils of the way, to urge upon us with all the affectionate solicitude of brothers and sisters, this childlike trust in the common Father of us all.

We hear them. We feel the force of their entreaties, Christ is with us all days even as He was with them. He asks us for our confidence, for His share of our troubles and our joys. He promises to care for all we entrust to Him.

And we cannot bring ourselves to commit ourselves wholly to Him with all that we have or desire—truly, "It is wonderful!"

X
AFTERWARDS

WE have reached a period in this terrific conflict when the end appears to be within measurable distance. After-war problems, bewildering in their magnitude and complexity, are occupying the minds of statesmen. How the engines of destruction this strife had brought into being may be so controlled as to protect the world against still greater horrors in the future; how existing relations between the Allies may be maintained and strengthened so as to be a guarantee for the world's peace; how its commerce is to be guarded; how political boundaries are to be readjusted according to justice and the legitimate aspirations of the smaller States; how the British Empire is to be reconstituted in view of the splendid loyalty and sacrifice with which the Dominions have come forward in its defence; how our men are to be cared for when they return from the trenches; how the industrial situation is to be met; and the whole question of the public position and influence of women in this country is to be settled—these are matters that may well occupy the minds of men at this crisis of the history of our race.

But there are others more important still. How this upheaval will affect the interests of God in the world of souls; whether the religious sense that has been aroused will develop, or be followed by a reaction and absorbed in a materialism for which new facilities will not be wanting; whether men will have learned a lesson from the Great War and will profit by the warning vouchsafed to them—this, too, is matter for speculation.

And lastly, we may wonder how long a course the reconstructed world may have to run. We can hardly fail "to see the signs of the times," to recognise in many of the evils now weighing upon men the calamities which our Lord tells us are to precede the end. Are these, we ask ourselves, "the beginnings of sorrows?" If men still ask: "Where are the signs of His Coming?" and their main concern is how they may buy and sell and plant and build as soon as the cannon's boom has ceased, do not the very stones cry out to us? What else is the meaning of the outstretched arms of the Crucifix which amid the ruins of Belgium and northern France the shells refuse to touch? What else is Notre Dame d'Albert doing as she bends with her Child over the stricken earth that He may see and pity?

In whatever way human affairs may settle down, we shall need more than ever the leavening force of religion to raise us above interests which are merely those of earth and time. The Church's daily call from every altar: "Sursum corda!" the ruins around us on every side, remind us that "we have not here a lasting city"; and in the very effort to build up the ruins we must remember that "we seek one that is to come."

In the meantime, our duties when the War is over will be many and pressing. More than ever will it be true that the women of a country make its history. How the millions of men discharged from the army, and the many hundreds of thousands of men and women discharged from munition work, are to find employment, is a problem to which no satisfactory solution at present offers. The "wave of unexampled prosperity" which the War has brought to the working classes cannot last. Depression will follow, and wide-spread distress and discontent. In many cases a family will have lost

THE STATUE OF OUR LADY ATOP
NOTRE-DAME DE BREBIÈRES IN ALBERT, FRANCE

The Church was heavily damaged in 1915 during the Battle of the Somme,
causing the statue to hang as shown until it finally fell in 1918.

its breadwinner. Some families have already so suffered, that neither husband, son, father, nor brother is left. The orphans of soldiers and sailors will be countless.

Women who "have responded nobly to the call that has come to them to take up new responsibilities and to enter on new professions" during the War must be ready for the no less onerous duties and responsibilities peace will bring. "For them will come the testing point when society begins its reconstruction."[1] There will be situations and problems innumerable in which only a woman's intuition, tact, and experience can meet the need. Life is by no means the uttermost our young men have given in this War. Many men will retain life, but shorn of all that to our human views makes life precious. It may be a life without consciousness, a life on a stretcher-bed, a life overshadowed by the crushing sense of uselessness. Men will return disfigured, maimed, helpless, a burden to themselves and to those they love. Will this second sacrifice on their part be of less account in the sight of God than the first? Will it not rather immeasurably heighten the first, and win for those who share their burden bravely a double crown?

It is to be hoped that the State, aided by charitable institutions, will be able to provide such material relief as will mitigate to some degree the rigour of these misfortunes. But unless private and personal endeavour come to the rescue, the aid will be miserably inadequate. We must bestir ourselves, one and all. These stricken men have given their all for us, and it will be our bounden duty to bring them and their families such assistance as Christian charity and self-sacrificing service make possible. Those who have themselves suffered loss may find here the opportunity of their lives, by throwing themselves into work for others which will save them from sinking down into the slough of morbid egotism. In the early stages of the

---

1   Lady Frances Balfour.

War we heard of ladies in France and Belgium who, having lost husbands or sons, turned their houses into hospitals and devoted themselves to the care of the sick and wounded. Opportunities of personal service, of giving food, clothing, care and love, will lie at every door. The only question will be how to organise effort and means, so that aid may be wise, prompt, and efficient. In the case of Catholic families, we shall have to be on the alert lest distress should imperil the children's faith, "much more precious," St. Peter tells us, "than gold tried by the fire."

All this will entail self-denial, readiness to work with others, self-effacement, patience, perseverance. But will these be wanting? With so many broken lives around us, lives broken in our defence and service, young lives freely offered by those who owe us nothing, will easy, self-seeking lives, which cannot exist without exciting pleasures and extravagant expenditure on dress and amusement, be possible amongst us?

What a statesman has said of the work before our politicians is true in its measure of all departments of social service, even of the village homes into which we may try to bring comfort and brightness: "There will be a variety of interests to harmonise, vehement passions to calm, reasonable ambitions to gratify, conflicting aims to reconcile, and friction to ease every-where. There has never been a conjuncture in the political history of Europe that required to a like extent the exercise of moderation, measure, forbearance, resourcefulness." We shall have to tax our ingenuity, our charity, and our patience to cheer the unnerved, the unmanned, the sick-at-heart, to lead them gently where alone true hope and comfort are to be found—in the faithful practice of their religion, in the Sacraments, before the altar of God. Happy shall we be if our own practice gives weight to our words; if from the abundance of the heart our words of consolation come, if our own suffering has brought

us that gift of real sympathy which those in sorrow are so quick
to detect and appreciate.

> Ask God to give thee skill
>   In comfort's art,
> That thou may'st consecrated be
>   And set apart
> Unto a life of sympathy:
> For heavy is the weight of ill
>   In every heart,
> And comforters are needed much
> Of Christ-like touch.

Early Christian traditions tell us that the desolation of the
Blessed Mother of God on Calvary was followed, after the short
period of the forty days of Christ's Risen Life, by a separation
which lasted for years, quite probably for many years. Think
where her heart was all that time! But she lived on here, and
was content to live—away from her Son, with John by her
side instead of Jesus, occupying herself, as "the handmaid of
the Lord," with the necessities of the early Church; instructing
and comforting the sorely-tried Christians; effacing herself
as of old; laying her hands to lowly household work like the
other women whose "labour in the Lord" St. Paul so gratefully
acknowledges.

And is not this what God will now ask of those who have
already made such sacrifice for His sake?—that they rise above
self-concentration and morbidness, and seek in labour for
others a solace for their own grief and the surest proof of their
love of Him? Whilst using the occasions Providence has ready
for us close at hand—the maimed and crippled from the war,
the instruction or amusement of children or young girls, the
comforting of the sick, the lonely, the aged whose work here
is nearly done—our service and our desires may go out to the
very ends of the earth. The Foreign Missions will have suffered
sadly from this terrible international conflict. Is there a greater
charity than to help on those who are toiling, alone and amid

difficulties we can hardly realise, in those far-off lands?

If our own sorrow has made us readier, at this time of general stress and affliction, to enter into the sorrows of others—"to feed the hungry, to clothe the naked, to counsel the doubtful, to comfort the sorrowful"—then, looking back from our place in Heaven on the troubles of the Great War, we shall own with thankful hearts that "to those that love God all things work together unto good."[1]

---

1 Romans viii. 28.

LAZARUS AND THE RICH MAN

by John Everett Millais

XI
"PLENTIFUL REDEMPTION"
"I believe in the Resurrection of the body."--Ps. xxix. 7.

WE say the words often, but do we at all realise how plentiful that Redemption is to be?

We think of it chiefly, and rightly, as it affects the soul, but the body, which for good or for evil is to be for ever the companion of the soul, is no less concerned. It is the entire man that has loved and served God, or outraged and set Him at naught. The entire man must therefore be rewarded or punished, according to his deserts.

St. Paul tells us that we "have received the spirit of adoption of sons, and if sons, heirs also...joint heirs with Christ, yet so if we suffer with Him, that we may be also glorified with Him." He goes on to say that "the sufferings of this time are not worthy to be compared with the glory to come that shall be revealed in us," and then adds, "the expectation of the creature waiteth for the revelation of the sons of God." Meanwhile, "we groan within ourselves, waiting for the adoption of the sons of God, the redemption of our body."[1] How earnestly he awaited this deliverance, this liberty, this complete redemption, we know from the cry: "Unhappy man that I am, who shall deliver me from the body of this death? The grace of God by Jesus Christ our Lord."[2]

St. Bernard in a beautiful parable puts before us the true relations of soul and body in this life. A certain prince, being

1   Romans viii. 15-23.
2   Romans vii. 24.

sentenced to a term of exile from his father's court, took up his abode with a poor widow, from whom he claimed shelter and sustenance. The fact that their needs and tastes were often at variance made it impossible for her to satisfy at once her royal guest and herself. But she knew her place and resolutely preferred his interests to her own. At length the exile came to an end, and he left her to enter into possession of his kingdom. There, presenting himself before the King, his father, he pleaded for her, saying: "I lodged heretofore with a certain poor widow, thy handmaid, who denied herself in many things that I might want for nothing. Seeing that now I am come into my own, I want her to be sent for to share my riches and my joy."

The happiness of the soul will not be complete till the body is called to share what it has helped to secure. That it may be a fit dwelling-place for a glorified soul, it will be endowed with certain properties which mediaeval theologians have enumerated for us under the headings of immortality, impassibility, clarity, and agility. The glorified Body of Christ is the model to which His members are to be conformed. "It hath not yet appeared what we shall be, we know that we shall be like Him"[1]—immortal, for "death shall be no more"[2]; free from all the ills of this life, "they shall no more hunger nor thirst, neither shall the sun fall on them nor any heat"[3]; glorious and beautiful; "then shall the just shine like the sun in the kingdom of their Father"[4]; able to pass at will through all substances, and to any place: "Jesus cometh, the doors being shut, and stood in the midst."[5]

"The adoption of sons," is no empty phrase. "Heirs of God and joint heirs with Christ" are titles which give us some idea of the liberty and glory of the children of God when they receive their inheritance in full. It is to fire his converts

1   I John iii. 2.
2   Apoc. xxi. 4.
3   Apoc. vii. 16.
4   S. Matth. xiii. 43.
5   S. John xx. 26.

with his own enthusiasm that St. Paul in his Epistles returns time after time to this central doctrine of the faith. He is preeminently the Apostle of the Resurrection. If St. Peter gives us the tremendous words: "Who is on the right hand of God, swallowing down death, that we might be made heirs of life everlasting,"[1] it is St. Paul who says: "For He must reign until He hath put all His enemies under His feet. And the enemy death shall be destroyed last."[2] There is no truth he preached more earnestly than the Resurrection of Jesus Christ from the dead and our resurrection as a consequence of His.

Men, nowadays, and women, too, are busy digging new foundations, seeking to attract the world by new revelations, instead of building on the old ones which faith provides. Even the faithful are sadly remiss in bringing home to themselves the truths which they believe. Women, we are told, do not analyse, they realise. However this may be, it is the realisation of the truths of faith that we need one and all in these days. And the realisation of the General Resurrection as much as any. It might be supposed that the overweening interest in the body which is such a marked characteristic of our times, would give the 11th and 12th Articles of the Creed an extraordinary fascination for us, and that we should ponder diligently the compensation for its present sacrifices in the interests of the soul, which awaits the body in the resurrection. But our inconsistency or our sloth prevents us from turning to account such a resource. The Resurrection of the body and Life Everlasting are details of our faith which we care neither to analyse nor to realise. Yet what an inexhaustible source of strength and consolation is here! Millions in every age have passed victoriously through all the trials of life; men and women all around us are bearing up with fortitude in these days of loss and separation, sustained by their unshaken faith in reward and joy to come: "I believe in the resurrection of the body and Life Everlasting. Amen."

1   I S. Peter iii. 22.
2   I Cor. xv. 25, 26.

Female Martyr

by Jacob van Oost the Elder

XII
JOY, PRAISE, SONG, THE LIFE OF HEAVEN

JOY. "I will greatly rejoice in the Lord, and my soul shall be joyful in my God, for He hath clothed me with the garments of salvation, and with the robe of justice He hath covered me, as a bridegroom decked with a crown, and as a bride adorned with her jewels."[1] "The bridegroom shall rejoice over the bride, and thy God shall rejoice over thee."[2] This is the fundamental joy of the soul as she enters Heaven. Not the fact that she has come to the end of her labours and is received to her reward. Not delight in any purely personal gain. She has reached salvation. O word which speaks of such a risk run, and of such a rescue! word which, seemingly negative, has been chosen by God himself to include all conceivable happiness; the absence of every cause of distress; peace, rest, the sense of safety and stability, the satisfaction of all just desires! She is saved. This is joy unspeakable. But there is a deeper still— that God is satisfied. That He who made her for Himself, and has been with her through dangers and struggle—all the long conflict with self, who in truest love and wisdom has subjected her at times to keen suffering, and has from first to last spent upon her so amazing an outlay of grace, that He is content with the issue, more than content. "Thy God shall rejoice over thee,

1   Isaias lxi. 10.
2   Isaias lxii. 5.

He will rejoice over thee with gladness."[1] The soul will rejoice that "clothed with the garments of salvation and with the robe of justice," she is pleasing in His sight, "as a bride adorned with her jewels."

As she enters the Heavenly Court, her eyes seek but one object—the King. "Thine eyes shall see the King in His beauty,"[2] is the promise that has sustained her through years of weary waiting and fears. The magnificence of that City of pure gold, with its gates of pearl, the dazzling glory of its inhabitants, these do not detain her. "Thou hast made us for Thyself, O God, and our hearts are restless until they rest in Thee."[3] "Show me Thy Face," she cries, "let Thy Voice sound in my ears, for Thy Voice is sweet and Thy Face comely."[4] I have found Him whom my soul loveth. I hold Him and will not let Him go. I will give praise to Thee, O Lord, with my whole heart, I will be glad and rejoice in Thee, I will sing to Thy name, O Thou Most High!"

Praise. This is the very breath of Heaven. The blessed are before the Throne of God. They see Him face to face. They see in Him Infinite Perfection— Holiness, Beauty, Joy, Wisdom, Love at their Source. How should they not praise!

They see the Wisdom which, reaching from end to end of our course on earth, orders all things sweetly. They see the Love that had us in mind, every one, during the long eternity when He dwelt alone; that gave us, in preference to others, a place in His world, and a work to do for Him which He will reward munificently when the time for reward has come. They see how He has planned our life and every detail of it with minutest care, leaving no room for chance; overruling the ill-will or mistakes of those about us, so that all may turn to our good and bring about the fulfilment of His designs. They see the Patience with which He bears our foolishness when

1   Soph. iii. 17.
2   Isaias xxxiii. 17.
3   St. Augustine.
4   Cant. ii. 14.

we mistrust Him; when we think that trial and trouble show He has forsaken us; when we cannot resolve to leave ourselves wholly in His hands. They see His Mercy in the forgiveness of our many sins; in the readiness with which He comes to our help whenever we call upon Him, nay, before we call: "Before they call I will answer; as they are yet speaking I will hear."[1]

They see in God as in a vast mirror all that it concerns them to know of what passes on earth. They see the Sacraments at work all over the earth, cleansing, strengthening, feeding, comforting the mystical Body of Christ. They see "from the rising of the sun to the going down thereof, sacrifice offered to His name in every place; the clean oblation"[2] foretold by the prophet Malachias; the perpetual Sacrifice going up to God from the altars of the Church. They see, without the veil which hides our Lord from us, Him who is there truly present, at once Priest and Victim—"Priest for ever according to the order of Melchisedech"[3]; "a Lamb standing as it were slain."[4] They see the grace of God flowing from Calvary, poured out thus in Sacraments and in Sacrifice upon the earth to-day. They see it upon sea and land, under the sea, and in the air; upon the battlefields, in busy cities, and in quiet homes. They see it snatching souls from hell at the last moment; giving contrition to the dying; guarding the innocence of children; guiding to God's Truth the simple and the upright whose only desire is to know and do His Will.

All this they see as they gaze upon God—how should they not praise Him!

Song. The soul of a people reveals itself in its native tongue. Enshrined there are its history, its character and its spirit, its tragedies and its triumphs. Do we desire to enter into closer relations with a nation, or to get a truer estimate of one which

1   Isaias lxv. 24.
2   Malach. i. 11.
3   Ps. cix. 4., Heb. v. 6.
4   Apoc. v. 6.

we have perhaps misjudged?—we take up the study of its language. If we fall out with a country, we forthwith boycott its tongue. The cruellest form of oppression is to forbid a conquered race the use of its native speech.

And all this is true of the language of Heaven, our native Land. We might have thought it would be forbidden to us here. But what has God withheld from us that would make for our happiness? "He that spared not even His own Son, but delivered Him up for us all, how hath He not also with Him, given us all things?"[1] Therefore, we are permitted to hear now and again stray harmonies from the heavenly Jerusalem. They rise above the gates of pearl and float down to us— faint echoes of the new song, the harping on the harps, the rise and fall of the eternal "Alleluia." It is not much, but it is a clue: "Holy, Holy, Holy, Lord God Almighty, who was, and who is, and who is to come."[2] "Give praise to our God, all ye His servants, and you that fear Him, little and great."[3] St. John heard the voices of the four mysterious living creatures, and of the ancients, of the Angels before the Throne, and of glorified human souls. "And they sung a new canticle...saying with a loud voice: The Lamb that was slain is worthy to receive power, and divinity, and wisdom, and strength, and honour, and glory, and benediction. And every creature which is in heaven and on the earth, and such as are in the sea, and all that are in them, I heard all saying: To Him that sitteth on the Throne and to the Lamb, benediction and honour and glory and power for ever and ever. Amen."[4]

What we notice about the speech of Heaven is, that it is all song and praise. Song—for how else could they bear the pulses that beat within their immortal spirits; the intensity of a life with every faculty at its highest; the face-to-face Vision;

1 Rom. viii. 32.
2 Apoc. iv. 8.
3 Apoc. xix. 5.
4 Apoc. v. 9, 12-13.

the vehemence of their joy; the white heat of their love? How could they bear it all but for the outlet in song? And therefore song ascends for ever and for ever before the Throne of God, except when, on a sudden, the singers pause—not weary, not satisfied, but hushed before some new-found beauty in God. "There was silence in heaven as it were for half an hour"[1]— the silence of rapt worship, and then, with fresh ardour, fresh jubilee, bursts forth anew that irrepressible praise.

---

1   Apoc. viii. 1.

In Mourning

by Charles Zacharie Landelle

XIII
PEACE

WE never knew its blessedness till now, when we are sending our nearest and dearest into the fiercest warfare men have ever known:

> While all about them rise
> The crashing discords of a world's dismay.[1]

The things of the next life are immeasurably beyond anything we can experience here. Yet we must try to realise them to some extent, and we may help ourselves by making use of the events, scenes and objects around us, those especially which forcibly strike the imagination, and, as St. Paul says, enable us by what we see to apprehend the unseen.

A conflict has been sprung upon the world which for magnitude and ferocity has no parallel. Everything about it is colossal. Earth is not wide enough, day not long enough for its hideous slaughter. Under the earth, on the sea and under the sea, among mountain crags where the dead lie, "unburied and unburiable," over peaceful homes at night, the struggle rages. Never have the evil passions of men been let loose to the extent we see to-day. Among savages of the most degraded races we look in vain for anything like it. On the other hand, the level of heroism displayed is so high and widespread that admiration becomes overtaxed and fails to respond at last to the calls upon it.

---

1 R.H. Benson.

Let us use these passing scenes to bring home to us eternal realities.

Do we feel our heart beating already in unison with that of a whole nation, with that of all civilised nations, with the heart of Humanity; in full sympathy with it; borne up by it, as we look forward to the day when a decisive action will at length close this disastrous war and bring about "the peace for which we long"? Then we may form some faint, very faint, idea of what it will be to be one of that immense multitude which with one heart and one soul will lift itself to God in the *Te Deum* of Heaven, that victorious close of all earth's conflicts and beginning of a blessed and eternal Peace.

As we think of our heroes leaving the trenches for good; of our prisoners freed from captivity and torture, on their way home; of the returning exiles of other lands; of the rebuilding of shrines and of homes; of the deliciousness of Peace; of the worldwide rejoicing—may we not pass on to the thought of the triumphal entries into Heaven, of the reunions there, of the freedom and the security "where the wicked cease from troubling and the weary are at rest"[1]?

Peace! Is it to be had even here? Yes, not in its fulness, but in its essence; in friendship with God, in conformity with His Will, by patient suffering and the earnest discharge of duty; in reliance on Him by prayer. But this supposes the unshaken foundation of religious faith. Hence the craving of so many of our men, as through their short term of training they advance towards the firing line, knowing what that line will mean to thousands, and may mean to them—for the faith which will bear them safely through the terrible ordeal and land them safely in eternity. They are sacrificing their all, and they plead for that compensation and support which is enjoyed by so many of their comrades—peace of soul, courage, assured hope in the face of death.

1   Job iii. 17

We all know the war with its attendant horrors has been the means of drawing back many souls to the practice of their religion. One of these, a young professor, happily married and the father of three children, was called to serve in the Army when the war broke out. He was a philosopher and a man of letters. He had ceased to be a Catholic, but his unbelief was a passing phase which he sincerely deplored. In October, 1914, he wrote a letter to his wife in which, after deliberately measuring the sacrifice that at any moment he might be called upon to make for his country, he adds: "Happy the believers!...They die for their God...they die with arms stretched out to the God who animates them...they die transfigured...I wish to return to the simplicity and openness that I admire so much in others." After having made his peace with God and received Holy Communion, he wrote again: "I am quite happy and at peace, as I never expected to be, given all that may happen to us here. I do not fear death. I am no longer alone. Pray that God may give me a living faith...I am learning to suffer." Before going into the engagement in which he was mortally wounded, he wrote to his wife: "I go into battle with a quiet conscience and a strong heart. I make the sacrifice of my life, not cheerfully, but deliberately."

The human touch in these letters makes them doubly valuable It adds an extra note of heroism to the calm, thoughtful, generous self-sacrifice of the noble soldier. He is an excellent specimen of hundreds of men of his generation, cultured and high-minded, but in whom the spirit of inquiry that characterises the present age has broken loose from the guiding hand of religious faith. Far from glorying in his unbelief, he suffered from it and in the sincerity of his heart prayed and sought for light. Suffering gave him the boon for which he craved; a strong living faith that did not take away the bitterness of the sacrifice, but that gave it a meaning.[1]

At a time like this, with wounds such as the Great War has brought, there must be no trifling; skilled hands only can be accepted. Nurses, stretcher-bearers, first-aid dressers, all must be qualified. But much more is skill called for when there is question of the precious life of the soul, of its wounds, of the way in which it is to be dealt with and cared for; there must be no trusting to chance, no bungling here.

The Catholic Church seizes a situation at once and adapts herself to it. In every conceivable emergency she knows exactly what to do and in the time at disposal. If there are minutes only, she has all essentials ready. To those unfamiliar with her

1 The *Catholic Times*, April 18, 1916

practised hand and methods, there is something marvellous in the deftness with which, all unadvised, she sets about and despatches vital and complicated cases. In her handling there is nothing tentative; all is sure, gentle, firm. The soul feels, and acknowledges in her, physician, nurse, and mother all in one, and gives itself up to her with the trust of a child. What wonder that men who have witnessed her dealings with souls cry out in their hour of need: "Why cannot we have what Catholics have when they go into action?"

Eighty thousand, we are told, die every day. We may think of the Church as a mother by many of these deathbeds, striving in prayer for souls in deadly peril; closing the eyes of old and young in peaceful homes; rocking on her breast, to soothe their piteous pain, the boys on the battlefield who call for "Mother" at the last.[1] Where she may, she will stand over the grave with her words of consolation and hope: "I am the Resurrection and the Life: he that believeth in Me, although he be dead, shall live." Nay—for we her children are one in faith and hope wherever death may find us—it is over all who call her "Mother" that she says these words as the grave closes over them. In this hope, with "Requiescat in pace," she lays them to rest as a mother her tired children, with the promise to wake them on the morrow.

Oh, that instinct with which the child turns to its mother in the last struggle! How it is showing itself at this time when, face to face with the realities of the next life, prejudice and doubts suddenly melt away, and the soul turns trustfully to the Church of all places and of all time for the succour she, and she alone, can bring! There are men, who have never given a serious thought to the "one thing necessary," now refusing to go

1   "After the battle, that day, you couldn't hear yourselves talk in the trenches for the cries of the wounded. It was like one great uninterrupted wail...Then little by little silence came, as a good many of them died. What we heard sound longest on the battlefield, from one end to the other, was the word 'Mother!' It is always those who are dying who call like that; we know that know."—*Letter from a war nurse.*

to the front except as Catholics! Others who in life have been content with a poor substitute cry out for their true Mother when they have death to face! No arguments, no persuasion are needed. Instinctively they call for her, recognise her, trust themselves to her.

ELIJAH RESTORING THE WIDOW'S SON

by Ford Madox Brown

XIV
"WOMEN RECEIVE THEIR DEAD RAISED TO LIFE AGAIN"
--Heb. xi. 35.

O NE of those tender phrases of Scripture which it is well to ponder at a time like this.

Women. Why are they singled out among a multitude of mourners as deserving of singular compassion and recompense? The words of Scripture are "justified in themselves," but we are encouraged to ponder them and seek out their significance. Why, then?

Because, perhaps, of their intenser affections, and therefore keener suffering? Or, as in this war, of their closer relationship with those whom death has claimed—brothers, husbands, sons?

Because of the self-restraint, the quiet heroism which home duties impose upon their grief? They have fewer of the distractions which relieve the burdened mind by changing the current of thought, and the nature of their employment being often such as to throw them back upon themselves, leaves them a prey to suffering in its acutest form—suspense or desolation.

Because of the helplessness which, as in this protracted struggle, can do nothing but suffer and pray and find its strength in silence and in hope?[1]—a helplessness which appeals powerfully to the compassion of our Heavenly Father, as we know by the frequent mention in Scripture of His care for widows and for orphans.

1   Isaias xxx. 15.

Because of the greater urgency of their petitions to God in behalf of those dear to them who are in need or in danger, and the trust with which they commit them to His protection and care?

For these reasons, it may be, Holy Scripture mentions, among mourners for their dead, Rachel, or again the heroic mother of the Maccabees, or the widow of Naim, or Magdalen and her companions, but above all the Mourner who, standing beside the Cross, can say with truth: "O all ye that pass by the way, attend and see if there be any sorrow like to my sorrow."[1]

Received their dead. Tender words, showing that their right survives death. As if their treasures, transferred to the treasury of God, were taken as a loan or trust, to be restored to them with interest in due time, the right to such restoration being acknowledged by God Himself.

"And when He came nigh to the gate of the city, behold a dead man was carried out, the only son of his mother, and she was a widow. Whom when the Lord had seen, being moved with mercy towards her, He said to her: Weep not. And he came near and touched the bier. And they that carried it stood still. And He said: Young man, I say to thee, arise. And he that was dead sat up and began to speak. And He gave him to his mother."[2]

Few passages in the Gospels set our Lord before us in a more tender light than this resurrection at the gates of Naim. His thoughts are centred on the mother. It is not the youth carried off in the flower of his age, nor the multitude who will spread "the rumour of Him throughout all Judea," nor the faith of His own disciples which the miracle will confirm, that moves Him to exert His power. But the bowed figure that follows the bier,

"Crumpling the pall up in her withered hands."

Those broken sobs, that helpless agony—it was this that

1 Lament. i. 12.
2 S. Luke vii. 12-15.

went to the Heart of the Son of Man. "Whom when the Lord had seen, being moved with mercy towards her, He said to her: Weep not...Young man, I say to thee, arise...And He gave him to his mother."

Their dead raised to life again. Seemingly so irrevocably lost, yet only taken for a while from the dangers and the horrors of this passing world, to be kept in safety for the resurrection and the eternal Day:

> All which I took from thee I did but take
> Not for thy harms,
> But just that thou might'st seek it in My Arms.[1]

Their own given back, and by what full restitution! God is so generous. He always gives more than He promises. He loves to repay by hundredfolds. "And the Lord blessed the latter end of Job more than his beginning."[2] He delights in glad surprises: "Jesus saith to her: Mary. She turning saith to Him, Rabboni!" He loves above all to reward trust: "Because he hoped in Me I will deliver him."[3]

And God loves to reward in kind. The faith that has trusted its treasures to His keeping shall receive them back, not as they were taken, but "clothed upon" with the glorious gifts of immortality, gifts that will not hide the identity which endeared them to us, or make them less our own than in the past, but only efface in the light of heavenly glory the blemishes of earth. With what delight shall women, shall mourners of this cruel war, receive their dead raised to life, for if it is to be by way of reward, it must be in the resurrection of glory that they are restored to them. They were taken away, frail, faulty, uncertain of their eternal lot. They are restored in the perfect beauty and integrity of the resurrection—Saints, confirmed in grace, more lovable, more loving, more our own than ever.

---

1   Francis Thompson.
2   Job xlii. 12.
3   Ps. xc. 14.

The Poem of the Soul:
Memories of Heaven

by Anne-Francois-Louis Janmot

XV
THE REUNIONS OF HEAVEN (1)

Tell us the things that are to come...
and we will set our heart upon them,—Isaias xli. 22.

IT is the perfect union of heart and soul among the Blessed that makes Heaven so truly Fatherland and Home. St. Paul speaks of the "weight of glory"[1] there, as if there were something almost oppressive in the magnitude of the reward. So may we think of the joy of each being so great that it can only be borne by being shared. "O magnify the Lord with me, and let us extol His name together,"[2] is the cry of every soul.

The "mine" and "thine" of earth has no place where love is perfected, where none are strangers but all part of one great family, because all are called and are indeed the sons of God.[3] "My Lord and my God!" "My God and my All!" is the cry of Saints on earth. In Heaven, as our Lord has taught us to say even here, it is: "Our God," "Our Father who art in Heaven." "Thou art worthy, O Lord our God, to receive glory, and honour, and power."[4] "Now is come salvation and strength and the kingdom of our God, and the power of His Christ, because the accuser of our brethren is cast forth."[5] "Alleluia. Salvation, and glory, and power to our God! Give praise to our God, all ye His servants, and you that fear Him,

---

1   II Cor. iv. 17.
2   Ps. xxxiii. 4.
3   I John iii. 1.
4   Apoc iv. 11.
5   Apoc. xii. 10.

little and great. And I heard as it were the voice of a great multitude, and as the voice of many waters, and as the voice of great thunders, saying, Alleluia; for the Lord our God, the Almighty, hath reigned."[1]

The joy and the triumph of one is the triumph of all, is seen in the countenances, is heard in the song of all. The coming of each soul to join that blessed company is a new joy to all. All are friends and comrades, bound together by ties stronger than those of kinship and friendship here. Though there are degrees in glory, all are worthy of the intimacy, familiarity, and love of the highest there. What joy will it be to be again in the midst of those who have fought the same fight with us, carried on the same work, persevered through the same difficulties, and are called now to share the same reward!

Yet within this rejoicing family there is an inner circle. The Holy Family of Jesus, Mary, and Joseph will acknowledge throughout eternity the sweet ties of earth. So will those who have formed the same home. Can we picture to ourselves their joy when that home is refound in Heaven never to be scattered again! What a Homecoming will that be, all the sweeter for the bitterness of the partings! What congratulations of fathers and mothers, brothers and sisters! What joy and admiration in their countenance and in their words as they look upon one another! As they hasten to meet and embrace us, we shall know them at once for our own. The dear familiar traits are there, and now with no flaw of human frailty. The old love is heightened by the new grace and beauty and tenderness every moment discloses. Oh, what faces lit up with gladness! What arms stretched wide to welcome us! What sense of delight as they crowd about us! What loving intercourse and happy questionings! And what thankfulness for God's mercies to us in the past—the ways in which He has led us, the perils from

1   Apoc. xix. 1, 5.

which His Providence has saved us! "He hath done all things well! He hath done all things well!" we shall cry in our joy and gratitude: "There hath not failed so much as one word of all the good things that He promised."[1]

We hear often of the desolation of Rachel, who will not be comforted because her children are not. But God does not leave her uncomforted: "Thus saith the Lord: Let thy voice cease from weeping and thy eyes from tears, for there is a reward for thy work...and there is hope for thy last end, and thy children shall return."[2]

To the weeping mothers of this time it shall be said: "Look about thee, and behold the joy that cometh to thee from God. For behold Thy children come, whom thou sentest away scattered, they come, gathered together from the east even to the west...rejoicing."[3]

See our dear men and boys as the Archangel's trumpet sounds over the battlefields of the Great War. "And the spirit came into them, and they stood up upon their feet, an exceeding great army,"[4] not for battle now, but for triumph, and rest, and reward; not for hate and death, but for love and life everlasting.

"O Death," we shall cry, as we see them coming, "O Death, where is thy victory? O Death, where is thy sting?"[5] "They shall no more hunger nor thirst, nor shall the sun fall upon them nor any heat. For the Lamb shall rule them and shall lead them to the fountains of the waters of life, and God shall wipe away all tears from their eyes."[6]

Would not one hour of such joy be recompense for the bereavement and loneliness now darkening our lives? But that hour of joy will never pass, and after millions of years will be as

---

1   3 Kings viii. 56.
2   Jer. xxxi. 16.
3   Baruch iv. 36, 37.
4   Ezek. xxxvii. 10.
5   I Cor. xv. 55.
6   Apoc. vii. 16, 17.

94

fresh and keen as in the first moment of reunion. This is only the beginning of God's reward.

> Alack, thou knowest not
> How little worthy of any love thou art!
> Whom wilt thou find to love ignoble thee
> Save Me, save only Me?
> All which I took from thee I did but take,
> Not for thy harms,
> But just that thou might'st seek it in My Arms.
> All which thy child's mistake
> Fancies as lost, I have stored for thee at home:
> Rise, clasp My Hand, and come!
> —Francis Thompson

XVI
THE REUNIONS OF HEAVEN (2)

IT is well to dwell on the reunions of Heaven, lest we be "sorrowful even as others who have no hope,"[1] because their faith in the promises of God is deficient. To bring home to ourselves the happiness in store for us when those we loved on earth are refound in Heaven, we have but to study our Lord as "the first-born from the dead,"[2] and see if we can find in His relations with those dear to Him any lessening of tenderness after His Resurrection. To satisfy His affection and hasten to His sorrowing friends, He reduced to the shortest span the three days in the tomb, and "very early on the first day of the week, while it was yet dark," He broke the bonds of death and was back among them, more loving, if possible, more attractive than before. See Him going in and out amongst His dear ones, leaving one party only to join another; promising an interview in Galilee at some undetermined time, and anticipating it immediately by showing Himself at least six times on the very day of His Resurrection; bringing to all the comfort all so sorely needed, with the special tenderness reserved for each. During the three years of the Public Ministry, there is no questioning the reality of His affection for His human friends. It is shown in human ways, by the need of personal presence, of sharing sorrows, joys, and dangers, of giving everything, even life itself, for the beloved. But after the Resurrection all this is more

1   I Thess. iv. 12.
2   Col. i. 18.

marked. No longer straitened by the baptism wherewith he was to be baptised, there is a joyousness about Him as of one whose life's burden has been removed. It is one trait more of likeness to us by which He endears Himself to us as the Son of Man. About all the appearances to His disciples during the forty days of His Risen Life, there is a simplicity and a homeliness which are perhaps their special charm. It was in homely intercourse with them that our Lord brought those who at first "believed not and wondered for joy,"[1] to realise that it was indeed Himself. He appeared to the Eleven "while they were at table," showed them His hands and His feet; offered Himself to be handled by them; asked them for something to eat, and took from their hands the broiled fish and honeycomb tremblingly laid in His. He prepared their meal on the seashore; "cometh and taketh bread and giveth them, and fish in like manner"; instructed, rebuked, and comforted them by turns. So dear to Him are these marks of familiar friendship that, speaking of His intercourse with His Elect after the General Resurrection, He says: "Blessed are those servants whom the Lord when He cometh shall find watching. Amen, I say to you, that He will gird Himself and make them sit down to meat, and passing will minister unto them."[2]

Not only, then, has He preserved the dear ties of earth, but He has taken them up again after death, strengthened, as is their wont, by separation. If our resurrection is to be modelled on His, we are surely bound to believe that the affections of earth endure where charity is perfected, and that one of the sweetest joys reserved for us hereafter is reunion with those we have loved here. He who has made the heart of man, and by experiencing its emotions in His sacred Human Nature has sanctified the joys and sorrows of family life, will give to those who have followed Him in the way of sacrifice the reward their

1   S. Luke xxiv. 41.
2   S. Luke xii. 37.

hearts desire. Our hearts, like His own, must be satisfied thus, if His promise is to be fulfilled: "Ask and you shall receive that your joy may be full."[1] "Your heart shall rejoice and your joy no man shall take from you."[2]

How will He Himself rejoice to satisfy the love of father and mother and children in the blessed reunion of the resurrection! How will He make them welcome to joys of which He can only say that "eye hath not seen, nor ear heard, neither hath it entered into the heart of man what things God hath prepared for them that love Him."[3] He will make them sit down to meat, and passing will minister unto them, pressing upon them all manner of delights: "Come, eat My bread, and drink the wine which I have mingled for you."[4] "Eat, O friends, and drink, and be inebriated, My dearly beloved."[5] "They shall be inebriated with the plenty of Thy house, and Thou shalt make them drink of the torrent of Thy pleasure."[6]

See them seated there. All so safe, so happy in the happiness of one another, so glad to be able to make Heaven happier for each. The day of toil and danger will be over, and we—weepers and mourners of this vale of tears—shall be Home at last!

There are those who look upon freedom from pain and distress, and reunion with those they loved on earth, as the main happiness of Heaven. They appear to desire nothing further, as if this would be absolutely satisfying throughout eternity. How little do they understand the vast capacity of the human heart and its insatiable cravings! He who made the heart knows that nothing but Himself can satisfy it. The joys to which we look forward so eagerly are not the essential joy of Heaven, which is the possession of God, the Source of all good

1 S. John xvi. 24.
2 S. John xvi. 22.
3 I Cor. ii. 9.
4 Prov. ix. 5.
5 Cant. v. 1.
6 Ps. xxxv. 9.

and of all joy. The sweet reunions there He gives us over and above. It is less to the other than the thin fringe of surf at the ocean's edge to the vast expanse beyond. If, then, this is such inexpressible delight, what will the Ocean be which is Himself!

> Ah, God is good, who writes His glory plain
> Above thee, and about thee at thy side—
> Bids thee look upward from that blinding pain,
> And, ere thy longing tires,
> Kindles His sudden fires.
> Look, and let all thy soul be satisfied!
>
> --R. H. Benson.

THE POEM OF THE SOUL: THE DIVINE GENERATION

by Anne-Francois-Louis Janmot

Additional titles available from

St. Augustine Academy Press

Books for the Traditional Catholic

Titles by Mother Mary Loyola:

Blessed are they that Mourn
Confession and Communion
Coram Sanctissimo (Before the Most Holy)
First Communion
First Confession
Forgive us our Trespasses
Hail! Full of Grace
Heavenwards
Holy Mass/How to Help the Sick and Dying
Home for Good
Jesus of Nazareth: The Story of His Life Written for Children
The Child of God: What comes of our Baptism
The Children's Charter
The Little Children's Prayer Book
The Soldier of Christ: Talks before Confirmation
Welcome! Holy Communion Before and After

Tales of the Saints:

A Child's Book of Saints by William Canton
A Child's Book of Warriors by William Canton
Illustrated Life of the Blessed Virgin by Rev. B. Rohner, O.S.B.
Legends & Stories of Italy by Amy Steedman
Mary, Help of Christians by Rev. Bonaventure Hammer
The Book of Saints and Heroes by Lenora Lang
Saint Patrick: Apostle of Ireland
The Story of St. Elizabeth of Hungary by William Canton

Check our Website for more:

www.staugustineacademypress.com